GETTING IT
TO THE BOTTOM LINE

GETTING IT
TO THE BOTTOM LINE

Management by Incremental Gains

Richard S. Sloma

THE FREE PRESS
A Division of Macmillan, Inc.
NEW YORK

Collier Macmillan Publishers
LONDON

Copyright © 1987 by The Free Press
A Division of Macmillan, Inc.

The Free Press
A Division of Macmillan, Inc.
866 Third Avenue, New York, N.Y. 10022

Collier Macmillan Canada, Inc.

Printed in the United States of America

printing number

1 2 3 4 5 6 7 8 9 10

Library of Congress Cataloging-in-Publication Data

Sloma, Richard S.
  Getting it to the bottom line.

  Includes index.
  1. Organizational effectiveness.   2. Performance.
3. Profit.   I. Title.
HD58.9.S56   1987   658.4'063   87–411
ISBN 0–02–929540–8

Having enjoyed a measure of success in business management, I dedicate this book to my four mentors, whose key insights guide me even to this day. I have been blessed with scores of solid business friendships. And, notable acquaintances, too, were made along the way: including Harold S. Geneen, Michael Blumenthal, C. Arnhold Smith, Victor Posner, and Bob Pritzker—to mention a few. But I will always hold my mentors in unique, warm regard.

These men will always occupy a special place in my mind and heart. In quiet moments, three of them share my reveries of the halcyon days when we made a favorable, measurable difference in the performance of our firms; when we made our "marks on the wall."

For good or otherwise, I am largely the result of the influences of the four men who have most affected my career.

1947   Paul Arthur Schilpp, Professor of Philosophy, Northwestern University

No one ever learns anything until he knows he has a problem.

1961–
1963   Robert S. Alexander, Vice President, Group Executive, ITT

You can do things graciously or ungraciously. It doesn't cost a nickel more to do them graciously!

1963–
1970   Arthur T. Woerthwein, Vice President, Group Executive, ITT

Always be "right," never be (merely) "logical." Time wounds all heels!

1970–
1975   Gordon Paul Smith, Chairman, CEO, Golconda Corporation

Seek, always ONLY excellence! Keep your integrity untarnished; it is your most important asset!

CONTENTS

LIST OF FIGURES

Chapter 1

What This Book Is All About
and Not About

This is a book about for-profit business management. It is *not* a book about leveraged buy-outs, mergers, acquisitions, or divestitures. It is not a book about how to become a millionaire with no money down. This IS a book about how to optimize operating profit in an ongoing business consistent with and supportive of the owners' (and/or creditors') demands.

This book is also (sadly) about perhaps a bygone time. You know, when the simple no-nonsense directives of "cut that out," "hush up," "go do that" were countered *not* with endless discussion but, rather, with spectacular and immediate results. I guess, if I were really pressed, I would admit that there is more profitability for the owners when there isn't preoccupation with process irrespective of result. Much more earthily put, communication was much more economical, clear, and compelling when, being told to "Eat your spinach," the kid (you and me?) just *did* it. Somehow it never occurred to me (did it to you?) that this was merely a negotiating point that we could subject to endless analysis and discussion, thereby avoiding the actual eating of the stuff. This is a book about EXECUTION.

The title of this book really says that it is concerned with business profits and profitability. And so it is. But a business posts a financial performance, whether excellent or otherwise, not because God so decrees it! It does so because the employees perform either excellently or otherwise. Of the three Ps in business—People, Product, and Plant—People is, of course, the most important. If both Product and Plant are excellent but the People perform only in a mediocre manner, the financial result will be mediocre. However, if both Product and Plant are mediocre but the People perform with inspired excellence, the financial result will indeed be excellent.

PEOPLE

This book is essentially about people; a special, well-defined group of people. This book is about business people, about the managers and supervisors who are responsible for the operating performance of the firm. Yet, it is also about the owners, the shareholders of the business, and the relationship between them and the management/supervisory group upon whom they must ultimately rely for achievement of operating objectives.

It should not be surprising that this book *is* about People because it is only through and by People action that financial performance of any kind is posted. It is generally agreed that the more dedicated and committed the management, the better the financial performance of the firm. If they merely contribute, the results will, at best, be only mediocre. What's the difference between "commitment" and "contribution"? Consider the ham-and-eggs breakfast that you had this morning. The chicken made a contribution, but the pig—the pig made a commitment!

You will find in this book a real-world tested and proven methodology for working with people in a professional manner to maximize their individual commitment to goal achievement. Don't be too surprised. This book was written by a professional manager who earned his stripes laboring in the trenches by running a firm. Too many (almost all) "fadsy" best sellers were written by guys who never ran anything!

This is also a book about individuals and individualism. It is a given that people always respond when they are treated as individuals, with individual needs, desires, dreams, and values; when they are treated with dignity and respect for their individuality. It was once said that the only way to make someone trustworthy is, in fact, to trust him. This book provides the wherewithal to treat people and their business performance on an individual, objective, and professional basis. If you want your employees to act with professionalism, treat each one professionally.

For a long time there has been disagreement after disagreement about how to deal with people in the workplace. On the one hand, there is the so-called humanist group which, in effect, maintains that privately owned, capitalistic firms should be managed principally for the benefit of the employees. They hold that it is the responsibility of the employer (the owner) to provide not only gainful, honest, and safe employment, but to provide all shades and types of social support as well. You know, drug rehabilitation, day-care centers, compensation based on "need" rather than on performance, and on and on. Their numbers seem to be, temporarily, increasing. I say temporarily because the number of adherents is bound to decrease. It is inevitable. Dissipation of profit will eventually take its toll in the form of diminished productivity, decreased or even negative growth, and, necessarily, decreased profitability.

On the other hand, there are also the "hell-bent-for-leather," insensitive guys. Too often their emotionalism and ego stroking result in subjectively defined policies, procedures, assignments, and objectives. Personnel are dealt with on a "whimsy and fancy" basis. People are hired (or fired, as the case may be) on the basis of such profundities as: "He (she) is (is not) our type of guy (gal)." Prejudice and bigotry are rife. "We really don't need to hire [substitute any or all of the following, or even some not included here: women, people over fifty, blacks, men, browns, Hispanics, Jews, Orientals, whites, Catholics, people under fifty, Baptists, and so on ad nauseum.]"

In summary, on the one hand, people are treated lovingly, paternalistically—womb-to-the-tomb sort of thing. They are treated as somehow inferior, deficient, or lacking. They do, however, know where they stand. They are led to believe that they are part of the "family," that they are and will be cared for by someone or some bureaucracy who really knows what's best for the poor darlings, don't you know.

On the other hand, some people never know where they stand. It all depends on how the "boss" feels today. They never know what is expected of them because nothing regarding their job is ever well-defined or measurable. They are always on the defensive—they can never, on their own, assert with confidence that they did, indeed, do the job that was expected of them.

The well-intentioned "bleeding heart" humanists treat people as though they were hapless, helpless corks, bobbing aimlessly amid the waves of the ocean of life. They need tons of TLC and a "Big Daddy" (whether the firm or the government) who knows what's best for them. The "subjectivists" tend to treat people with cold, calculated indifference. In their eyes, people are economic *and* psychological commodities; people were put on earth to be exploited by the "superior" owners and to practice mindless subserviance.

So ends a too-brief summary of the two polar extremes of people-managing schools of thought. Where does Management by Incremental Gains fit in? It strikes the long-sought-after logical balance of viewing and managing people as if they were competent, conscientious, and ambitious individuals who genuinely seek opportunities for professional growth and development. It provides treatment of individuals with the greatest degree of respect; it accommodates both the generation of optimal profit and return on investment for the owner/employer *and* the high levels of dignity to which all individuals are inalienably entitled. Measured performance levels, objectively set. Performance counts—irrespective of gender, color, race, national origin, religious preference, or whatever. People know explicitly what is expected of them and are provided with the wherewithal to measure and report on their own, individual progress. Not only is opportunity for personal development provided, it is expected! Not only is incremental compensation available for incremental performance, it becomes a contractual entitlement as each individual performs and earns it. Measures of performance competence and professionalism are quantified, impersonal, objective, and independently measurable for *each* individual. Incremental rewards are earned as individual performace meets/exceeds *that* individual's objectives, irrespective of the performance of his peers, of the other members of the management group.

Management by Incremental Gains places a great burden on the chief operating officer, the general manager, or president—whomever is in charge and responsible for operational performance. He must lead! He must be a "pro." He must have genuine respect for the right of people to be treated as individuals. He must want to maximize the enduring value of the shareholders' investment. He must want the individuals in his organization to grow, develop, and prosper in proportion and commensurately with their actual performance.

In summary, the aim of this book is to teach individuals *how* to fish, rather than merely, charitably, provide fish for the "needy." It shows people how to stand on their own two feet, to take rightful pride in a job well done, to be self-sufficient, to grow, to develop, to earn a higher standard of living for the owners and for themselves.

NUMBERS

But this book is also about numbers. Not just any kind of numbers. We're going to deal with financial and operational performance numbers. Essentially, there are two types of numbers: Plan Numbers and Actual Numbers. You will find that the most useful format and methodology for planning and controlling includes both the Income Statement and the Cash Flow Statement. As you become familiar with these formats, you will discover that they provide two essential components of a vector: measured *magnitude* and *direction;* and how much and the relative improvement over run-rate or prior levels. These two components, simply stated, measure the magnitude and direction of the planned changes in financial and operational performance.

The level of performance excellence achieved in any firm is a function of the sum levels of performance of all the individual people in that organization. The "magnitude" and "direction" of incremental performance excellence are quantitatively provided by the formats. The methodology, and procedures to optimally utilize these formats are presented later.

The "sense" component is provided by people, and there are two principal elements which comprise this component. Both are attempts to evaluate and judge the "sanity" of the proposed action or objectives. Both ask whether what we're proposing to do or planning to do is realistic, is "doable." The first element of the "sense" component is the evaluation of the minimum acceptable performance levels as defined by the owners and/or creditors. Does what the owners/creditors minimally expect of the firm have reasonable likelihood of achievement? If there's no viable chance of producing what is only minimally acceptable, it's better to get out while the exit is still voluntary.

The second element of the "sense" component is the

evaluation, the sanity-check of the do-ability of the performance objectives required to meet the minimal performance levels earlier established by the owners/creditors. Have we got the brainpower and the horsepower to make it happen? Do we have the requisite quantity and quality in our organization? If not, do we know specifically what we need and can we get it in time? This is the best time to present the conceptual framework of this book, as illustrated by the following eight steps.

Step 1: Quantify the Do-Nothing Scenario

The purpose or output of this first step is to obtain an evaluation of the likely future financial results for the firm if no substantive operating changes are made. It is, essentially, an extrapolation of the run-rate that the firm has posted in the relatively recent past. One important refinement of the run-rate forecast is the adjustment for any significant development, favorable or not, which is "known" to eventuate during the forecast period.

This step is discussed and analyzed in detail in three different contexts in Chapter 6 ("Operating Pre-Tax Profit"), 7 ("Operating Cash Flow"), and 8 ("Employee Compensation Costs/Expenses").

Step 2: If It Works, DON'T Fix It

We learned that the Do-Nothing scenario projected results which actually were acceptable to the owners/creditors, can you believe it? I guess once in a blue moon that may happen. If that *is* the case, do nothing to change the operating environment, at least during the forecast period. What you should do is examine and quantify those causal, underlying elements of forecast performance to determine (a) their likely duration, and (b) how their favorable effect can be enhanced and/or made even more enduring. *The idea is to try to continue to do more of that which we are already doing well.* So long as the run-rate forecasts are acceptable, don't muck around trying to do things if you really don't know that you can do it at least equally as well as what you have done and are doing. Whew! That's a tough sentence, but I think you get the point. It should be obvious that the two principal, if not exclusive, ingredients of financial and operations performance progress are: people and numbers.

Step 3: Quantify the Minimal
Acceptable Performance Levels

We have learned that the run-rate forecast is not satisfactory to the owners/creditors. That's almost always the case. It matters only in degree whether the unacceptability stems from outright losses or "only" unacceptably low levels of pre-tax profit and cash flow. The essential point is that the owners/creditors are *not* happy! So, operating management must *do* something.

The first thing that must be attained, if financial and operational performance improvement is seriously sought, is complete, useful communication by the owners/creditors to the operating management of specifically what performance levels are minimally acceptable. The owners/creditors should document *both* the requisite financial results *and* the on-or-before date by which those results must be posted.

The Financial Performance Objectives spelled out by the owners/creditors must, first of all, be realistic. I do *not* mean "conservative," as do many people when they say "realistic." What they really mean is, "Please lower the goal. I don't really want to feel vulnerable." What *I* mean by realistic is the lowest performance level at which the owners/creditors are indifferent to alternate investment alternatives. In other words, I mean financial performance at a level such that the *total* return to the owners, both financially and (perhaps more important) *non*financially or psychic, meets their "Do not liquidate and reinvest" test.

It has often been said that money itself is the only economic commodity that does not generate diminishing value as quantity increases, does not conform to the law of diminishing return. In other words, there are countless cases where owners value dollar number two million and one just as much (and many times even more) as dollar number two million. So, if the run-rate forecast displays results already above the "Do not liquidate and reinvest" threshold, and absent directives from the owners to the contrary, the objectives can and should be set at even higher levels.

In any event, performance excellence will be precluded if the objectives fail to demand "stretch." Adopt the "Star-Trek" mentality. Demand that operating management reach new, more rewarding higher performance levels, that they boldly go where the firm has never been before.

The methodology for defining pre-tax requisites is presented in detail in Chapter 6. The definition of cash flow requisites is the subject matter of Chapter 7. The consequential required changes of employee compensation costs/expenses are discussed in detail in Chapter 8.

Step 4: Quantify Components of the Financial "Performance Gap"

The "performance gap," or the challenge to operating management, is, essentially, the difference between the Minimal Acceptable Performance as quantified in Step 3, and the quantified Do-Nothing Scenario from Factor 1. For example, the Do-Nothing Scenario may indicate that an operating pre-tax of $100,000 and cash flow of $125,000 will be generated in, say, the next six months. If cash outflow for debt service and other nondelayable requirements amount to $200,000 over the same six-month period, then the performance gap amounts to $75,000 worth of positive cash flow that must somehow be generated if the firm is to survive. Many actions can of course be taken to improve both the quantity and the quality of the pre-tax and cash flows over any given time period.*

The computational task of this step is a deceptively simple one. Merely subtract what the results would be if we made no changes in the operating environment from what is minimally acceptable to the owners/creditors. Just how high *is* the firm's survival threshold?

---

* For complete "how to" details, please refer to THE *Turnaround Manager's Handbook*, Free Press, 1985.

Step 5: Cut Your Losses, Liquidate, and Reinvest Elsewhere

A quick sanity check of the measurements made in Step 4 tells us that there is no way we can achieve the minimal acceptable levels of performance or even come close! The survival threshold is just too high.

It's really a sad state of affairs because the result tells us that just about everybody connected with the operating management of the firm was asleep at the switch—and not just for a little while. While it's too bad, there's no sense, as they say, crying over spilt milk. Cut your losses. Liquidate. Reinvest elsewhere. But, for Christ's sake, learn from your experience so you won't repeat it.

Step 6: Quantify Management Action Plans to Bridge the Performance Gap

To get to this step, we will have already learned that while do-ability of the operating management challenge is definitely not out of the question, we're not yet sure that likelihood of achievement of minimal acceptable performance is appreciably better than 50–50 to warrant forbearance of liquidation action.

The computational task of this step is the anatomization of the total performance gap. That is, if, say, the pre-tax gap is $100,000 in total, operating management must ascertain each portion of the total goal that is logically assignable or delegable to each respective operating function—namely, sales, marketing, purchasing, production, engineering, and so on.

Chapter 5 supplies an abbreviated treatment of profit planning and the planning process. Chapters 6, 7, and 8 provide the format and methodology with which to (a) splinter the total goal among the operating functions and, thereby, (b) establish meaningful personal accountability of material and relevant performance quanta.

In brief, the OPS approach will be emphasized and elaborated. Objective/Problem/Solution—that's what OPS stands for. First, define the Objective, then, with equal care, define the Problem (the obstacle that *prevents* you from reaching your Objective; in other words, you would already have achieved the Objective BUT FOR . . .). Finally, state, quantitatively, what you plan to do to overcome the obstacle, to solve the Problem so that the Objective will be achieved.

Step 7: Define, Establish Reporting and Control System

Effective reporting and control is analyzed and discussed in detail in Chapter 9. The key principles which govern and maximize effectiveness of the reporting and control system are highlighted below.

First of all, the reports should always be comparative. And, further, *the comparison should always be made between what actually occurred and what was planned to occur.* That is not to say that actual-to-plan should be the only comparison. The mission or purpose of reporting is to inform, communicate, and provide insights—provide factual bases from which logical and useful inferences can be correctly drawn. Therefore, any and all comparisons which advance that purpose should be used. After all, the key questions that we need answers to are:

A. Did we perform as we planned to?
B. If we did:
   1. Where, specifically, did we excel?
   2. Why did we excel?
   3. How much more should we plan to do? How much higher can objective performance levels be realistically set?
C. If we did not perform as we planned to:
   1. Where, specifically, did we fail?
   2. How bad is the shortfall? How far off the mark are we?
   3. Is the failure remedial in the time remaining? If so, what is the recoup plan?
   4. Is it remedial at all? If not, how bad is the impact on the firm's total performance? Can the shortfall be made up in another way within the same organizational function? Or, can it be recouped in another function? For example, if the Objective was to achieve a specific level of gross margin dollars and it appears that insufficient quality and quantity of order intake will be forthcoming in a timely manner, can those pre-tax dollars be made up within the Sales Management function by, say, reducing expenses? Or, in the alternative, can Manufacturing Management supply the needed pre-tax dollars by reductions in burden, labor, or material costs/expenses?

These are management questions. They require management answers. Effective reports, then, are management reports, *not* accounting reports. What are the central implications of that assertion?

A. Data sequence control should focus on amount fields rather than account number and subaccount number fields. Thus, amounts are presented in descending sequence so that the user-manager never need worry that there are crocodiles hiding in the weeds further down the river. Maximize the benefits of Pareto's Law (you know: 80 percent of the action is generated by 20 percent of the actors). Go where the action is—*not* the actors!

B. The percent difference of the comparison of actual-to-plan should always be computed and reported. The user-manager may even find it useful to get the report printed in ascending sequence of percent. Thus, minus percents or performance shortfalls head the list in descending sequence of severity. Again, the manager's learning and review task is facilitated—he gets the worst of the bad news first.

C. Bad news—that is, performance shortfalls from plan—should be reported as soon as possible. The effectiveness of remedial action is enhanced as operating management learns not only the extent of the shortfall, but learns of it early enough to initiate remedial, restorative action.

    To help you remember this point, never forget the doctor who called his patient at 11:00 P.M. one evening and said, "I have some bad news and I have some *really* bad news. Which do you want first?'' The patient, aghast, said, ''The bad news.'' The doctor replied, ''The bad news is that you have only one day left to live. The *really* bad news is that I should have called you yesterday.''

D. Many of the measurements for both planned objectives and related actual results are data which are (and should be) outside the accounting system—pounds shipped, line items per order, line items per invoice, population, and so on.

Reliance on ''physical'' data in addition to ''fiscal'' data is not only warranted, but desirable for two basic reasons: (1) Early reporting is enhanced. We don't have to wait for the books to close, etc. And (2) tangibility of planned objectives/actual results enhances understanding of the performance and facilitates inspection and control.

E. The scope of the report should be limited to the sphere of cognizance and responsibility of the person whose performance is being reported upon. This is another way of saying that all Performance Objectives should be personally assumed, assigned, or delegated.

F. The quantity of reports supplied should reveal actual-to-plan comparisons of *all* of the report recipients' Objectives. First, this means that all the performance objectives should be quantified, measurable, and not subjective. Second, this point and E above combine to say that every manager whose performance is being reported upon should receive comparative data for his personal objectives as well as for his performance objectives.

Step 8: Define, Implement an Incentive Compensation Program

As with Step 7 above, the detailed analysis and discussion of this step are presented in Chapter 9. The following items highlight some key points and criteria relative to an effective Incentive Compensation Program.

A. There should be no performance objectives which are not suitable *and used* for incentive compensation purposes. This is another way of saying that all performance objectives should require performance above the level of that required to satisfy Job Description responsibilities and duties.

B. There should be no management imposed limit or "cap" on the amount of incentive compensation that can be earned.

C. The fundamental keystone of every effective Incentive Compensation Program is the principle that Performance Objectives and incentive compensation earned for meeting/exceeding those Objectives are personal, individual matters. We like to echo the conventional wisdom, for example, that accountability reporting is a desirable feature of an accounting system. We like to say that the Chart of Accounts should be defined and tailored to provide the ability to closely measure data under the control of the respective individuals. Why, then, do we encounter opposition to also paying incentive compensation on an individual basis, irrespective of performance elsewhere in the firm?

The answer, I fear, is neither very pleasant nor very comforting. Opposition to the concept of allowing each individual to earn in proportion to and commensurate with his own personal, individual performance exists to the degree that higher-level management abdicates and abrogates its leadership role and responsibilities attendant thereto. They simply lack the professionalism to face up to the admittedly difficult challenge of setting objectives properly and prudently. They unfoundedly and excessively fear that somehow the program will slip from their control and result in unfair or windfall payments to some individuals. Nobody said that anticipating the results would be easy. But while the anticipatory and foreseeability aspects of incentive compensation objective setting *are* difficult, they are not insurmountable. In too many cases, higher-level management is simply too lazy or too incompetent, or some combination thereof, to perform their monitoring and review evaluations in an effective professional manner.

D. Each participant in an Incentive Compensation Program should be able to track and measure his own performance and his rewards therefor.

E. Very, very few functions, developments, circumstances, events, and so on, can really be "controlled" by a participant in the Incentive Compensation Program in the long run. Too often, this so-called lack of control is cited to excuse poor performance or performance shortfalls. "Too often" because in the relatively short term of a fiscal year, if the performance objectives are reasonably set, the participant does indeed exercise control over his incentive compensation destiny.

F. An Incentive Compensation Program should never be
    a substitute or a subsidy for ordinary compensation.
    Be competitive in the management labor market only
    with ordinary compensation elements—for example,
    salary, percs, benefits, etc.

    Use an Incentive Compensation Program to attract
    and retain the really talented and aggressive personnel
    who have the wherewithall to really improve the firm's
    performance.

You will find the insights of Chapter 4 particularly useful
and rewarding. Management by Incremental Gains provides
the underlying rationale for this book. *At root is the recognition that results occur whether they are favorable or not,
never a bunch at once—always a little at a time.* A bucketful
does not magically appear one Monday morning. Rather,
it becomes full (or empties if there is a hole in the bottom)
drop by drop by drop.

Another cardinal notion presented here can be cogently
described as parametric "sensitivity." To gain insight into
the workings of this notion, view the posted financial results
of the firm as parameters of performance, as boundaries
of financial behavior. Perhaps a specific example will
help.

It is widely accepted that there is a nexus between market
share and product price in a competitive market. We can
begin with this conventional wisdom and proceed to explore
the relationship and its implications regarding management
strategy one step at a time. Thus, to improve operating
cash flow and profitability, management can, systematically, raise prices by an amount small enough to (largely)
avoid a "take them off the vendor list" reaction, yet large

enough to more than offset the expense of announcing and administering the price increase.

The idea is that, in general, as you raise prices you lose some market share. That is very often a good deal for the firm if not carried too far. Suppose that sales are $500 and the firm has been making 10 percent pre-tax profit, or $50. Let's assume that we lose 1 percent of share or 1 percent of volume for each 1 percent increase in price. Now, let's raise the price by, say, 5 percent. What happens? Well, sales drop by 5 percent, from $500 to $475, on which we still earn our historic 10 percent pre-tax, or $47.50. Then, even though we raised the price by 5 percent, sales return to the $500 level, BUT all of the price increase of $25 drops directly to pre-tax. Pre-tax grows from $47.50 to $72.50! Thus, while sales dollars have remained essentially the same, pre-tax jumped from $50 to $72.50, an increase of 45 percent!

The owners certainly don't want us operating managers to lose too much volume or market share. Not to worry. We won't let it get out of hand. First of all, price action *is* reversible. What went up yesterday can come back down next week. The market won't let us get away with raising prices too often, but then the incremental price increases will not be all that large to begin with.

Second, keeping tabs of the Gross Margin Content of the Forward-Aged Order Backlog should usually give us enough early warning to avoid serious harm.

A synonym for Management by Incremental Gains is Management at the Margin. In other words, the focus of management concentrates on the increment of change generated in financial performance by a quantum of change in operating conditions. Okay, what in the world is a quantum of change? Well, what I'm trying to describe is a distinguishable and measurable unit of management action. For an example of a quantum of change, refer to the earlier cited price increase action. The quantum of change in that case would be defined as "Raise prices on Product Lines 1, 2, and 4 in Channels 2 and 6 by, respectively, 2 percent, 4 percent, and 3 percent to take effect no later than (date)." We could go a little further and spell out the way the price increase should be implemented: change list price, change discount schedule, alter freight allowance, etc., etc. And we should identify who has the responsibility for effecting the change.

Effecting change, of course, is the basic underlying purpose of operating management. The emphasis on "effecting" provides insight into its nature. *It is always the task of operating management to take the firm from one performance level to another, higher, more acceptable level.*

Among the consequences of this basic mission is the need to execute actions that have not been tried before, to do things differently. Hand in hand with this leadership role goes the disproportionately extensive exposure to Monday morning quarterbacking, to second guessing. However, every successful operating manager must have already learned to be comfortable while vulnerable.

Both the nature and purpose of operating management are presented in detailed discussion in Chapter 3.

Yes, this book is about all of those things. But it's also about something far more profound. It's about a new management theory and the postulates that support and explain it. And to close the loop, it's about a time-tested, real-world-proven quantitative formulation, the use of which will consistently result in successful management performance.

Implementing Management by Incremental Gains is presented in three principal business segments or contexts. It is applied to effecting change in the operating pre-tax statement in Chapter 6, the operating cash flow statement in Chapter 7, and performance improvement of employee compensation costs/expenses in Chapter 8. In Chapter 9, the loop is closed: management reporting and control techniques cap the planning techniques in Chapters 6, 7, and 8. You've got it all: planning and control.

MANAGEMENT BY INCREMENTAL GAINS

This section begins, in Chapter 2, by exploring what the owners really want and why they really want it. In Chapter 3, our focus turns to operating management. These are the people, after all, who ultimately must perform and execute the plans and programs to meet the demands of the owners. Then, in Chapter 4, the concept of Incremental Gain is presented. Finally, in Chapter 5, the essentials of effective business profit planning relate and tie together the earlier three basic ingredients: owners, management, and the techniques for managing by incremental gain.

Do not omit study of this section. It will equip you to understand the causal forces and motives, the *whys* that make Management by Incremental Gain relevant, legitimate, and virtually universally applicable.

Ten words of ''why'' are worth a thousand words of 'how.''

Chapter 2

What Do the Owners Really Want?

What *do* the owners really want? Do they all want to maximize their financial return on investment in the near-term? "No" is a safe answer. In the long term? "No" again. Each owner and/or owner group has a somewhat different goal than another owner or owner group.

So, before operating management can go forth and effectively discharge its responsibilities, learning what the owners really want is an absolute necessity. It will not be easy. Very seldom do the owners themselves know what they really want. And even in the rare case when they do, they are notoriously inept at describing it with anything even remotely approaching clarity or definition.

What this chapter discusses is the many and varied owner-want alternatives. If you're an owner, carefully read this chapter so you can more effectively and economically lead your operating management. If you're a member of operating management, carefully study this chapter so you can more easily read the signs and discern the wants of the owners so that, in turn, you can better fulfill your managerial duties and responsibilities. But before we get into those topics, let's assume a case where the owners' wants are just not known or knowable in a reasonably short time period. In such a situation, there's only one thing you can do.

On your own initiative, set the Minimal Acceptable Pre-Tax Performance level far enough above the run-rate forecast to constitute a realistic operating challenge. Why concentrate on pre-tax? Simple. If operating pre-tax is negative, whatever cash flow there is must represent conversion of assets, including deferred expenses, into cash. It is reflective and indicative of liquidation of the firm. And if operating pre-tax is only inadequate, then cash flow, too, must be inadequate.

Before we begin to delve into detail, let's get a couple of things straight about owners and my attitude toward owners. Let's start with my attitude, OK? It's simple, basic and down-to-earth. Aside from complete, total and all encompassing envy, I have no feelings for them at all!! That's it! As Peggy Lee made famous a few years ago, "Is that all that there is?" YES!

The most important thing to remember about owners is the Golden Rule: He who has the gold, rules! And that, my friends, is that! There's really no need to explain why it behooves management to try to do that which the owners want, is there? I mean, self-preservation, job continuation, and all that, right? Okay then, let's proceed.

Don't forget, ever! Owners have the *right* to NOT try to maximize financial return on their investment! It may require too harsh an approach to employees for their taste. That's okay! Or it may mean they can't play "Big Daddy" anymore! And that's okay, too! They *do* own the joint!

CLOSELY HELD: WIDELY HELD

The first ownership characteristic deals with the different role and effect that wants, needs, and wishes of the owner play, and this depends upon whether ownership is closely or widely held. There is a third variation, namely, when one shareholder holds control and there are many other shareholders who each own relatively few shares and the firm is publicly traded, we usually call it a privately held, publicly owned corporation. As far as the owners' wants, needs, and wishes are concerned, this type of corporation most closely resembles a closely held firm.

When ownership or even control rests with one individual, his needs and wants will most likely be characterized by a stated shorter time period and will change, sometimes considerably, over time. He will have debt service requirements to meet *this* month or next. Next year? Hell, let's worry about that eleven months from now! What? You really expected something different? C'mon. Nothing changes much even from high school days. If the term paper is due May 15 and it's now January 4, you can bet your bippee that serious work on it won't begin until May 10 (if you're conscientious), or May 14 (if you're normal). After all, owners are individuals who are not all that different in many ways from any other individuals.

Figure 1 illustrates the relationship between the number of shareholders needed to exercise control and the expressed personal subjectivity content of the owners' wants, needs, and requirements.

The nature of this relationship should not be surprising. It does, however, provide useful insights for the ''non-

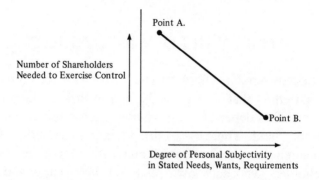

Figure 1.   Shareholders/Subjectivity

family-related'' manager who is conscientiously trying to run the firm according to the desires of the owners. If, for example, you're dealing with a firm at point A, the owners' needs, wants, and requirements can almost be completely discerned by imagining yourself in his shoes. *The most useful place to begin is to consider the concept of "psychic income."* Psychic income is fulfillment of that sense of self-satisfaction or of a psychological need(s) such that it is acceptable to the owners in lieu of hard cash financial return. Psychic income is always a ''deduct'' from financial income. Such decidedly personal and individual needs and preferences range all the way from (a) the value of having an office to go to every morning to (b) playing Santa Claus by personally giving a substitute as you see fit (turkey, ham, basket of groceries) to each employee from time to time. And there are all sorts of individual eccentricities in between.

REMEMBER: Your job, as an employee-manager, is not *to judge whether you feel that the owners' needs and preferences are worthy or otherwise; it is, first, to ascertain as*

definitively as possible what the owners' needs and prefer-
ences are *and, second, to develop programs and plans*
that will meet as many of these needs and preferences in
as short a time period as practical.

Being at Point B means that you will be faced with a
more complex task of trying to meet owners' wants and
needs than if you were at Point A. This is primarily true
because you're dealing with (trying to deal with) the *ego*
of a single individual who is not used to being told, "No."
Generally, these people march to a drum different from
the one which sets the cadence for the "hired gun," "non-
family-related," "professional" manager. I once knew a
shareholder who exercised control not because of the size
of his holdings, but because of the lack of harmony and
unity among the principal family member shareholders.
His ego drive led to the acquisition of a totally unrelated
and irrelevant electronics firm—despite the fact that he
knew nothing about electronics! He was the only one in
his clique at the club who was *not* involved in electronics.

The best indication of what the owner at Point B wants
is the array and extent of personal goodies that he has
enjoyed in the past; the more recent the past, the more
relevant they are. Is his ego stroked by a sumptuous office?
Then arrange to have it decorated with original works of
art. The owner will find that merely meeting with a designer
who asks about *his* taste and preference in art is quite a
trip all by itself. Does he and/or the members of his family
like to travel internationally? Okay, then set up distributor/
client/customer meetings at the off-shore locations and times
that are most conducive to the owner's needs. And, of
course, be sure to institute policy which authorizes first-

class travel for any trip in excess of, say, one hour's duration for all personnel who happen to be both an officer and a director. For good measure, you might as well throw in the same provision for all members of that officer/director's party. Help to document Deferred Compensation Agreements, "Golden Parachutes" if the firm is to be sold (see "Cash-In" alternative later in this chapter), and so on. In general, start by trying to provide the owner with all of the amenities and services you, in your "heart of hearts," would really like.

The approach from Point A is considerably different. The more remote, physically and financially, the shareholder is, the more he is interested in either of one of two things. If he's young, he is primarily interested in a steady increase in the enduring value of his investment. If he's elderly, he's far more interested in the size and reliability of dividend payments, the security of his income stream.

There are always exceptions, of course. But if you have no hard data to lead you elsewhere, this will give you an approach that will "guarantee" a 95 percent correct, relevant, and appropriate management approach.

Finally, you will, on occasion, run into high-level managers at Point A who act as though they are the owners in a Point B context. They act as if they own the place! They run it for their personal gratification rather than that of the shareholders. Waste no time trying to meet *their* demands or needs. Time wounds all heels and they will sooner or later be held to account. And when that moment arrives, you're far better off to be disassociated from them.

For any and all cases where there is an absence of specific direction to the contrary, enact those programs and projects which enhance the enduring value of the investment of *all* the shareholders. *You will never go wrong!* Time will be on your side. You will not have precluded other options or alternatives.

RETURN ON INVESTMENT (ROI)

This want, need, requirement gets an awful lot of traffic. Let's maximize ROI (for Christ's sake!). Let's optimize ROI! Too much emphasis is placed on short-term ROI results and not enough on short-term ROI performance. Forget ROI! What's our Return on Net Worth (RONW)? Forget RONW. What's our Return on Assets (ROA)? Or our Return on Tangible Assets; or . . . and so on.

Assume that every firm you encounter is maximizing ROI! Why not? If, say, reasonable alternative investments yield 14 percent and the firm is booking only 9 percent, how can anyone in their right mind say the firm is maximizing ROI? Very easily, is my reply. Recall our earlier discussion of psychic income? Well, in the case at hand, psychic income amounted to, precisely, 5 percentage points of ROI. Think about it a moment.

Assume that the owners' holdings could be liquidated intact and reinvestment at the 14 percent level could be made ex-fees or other charges. Normally, a prudent, cold, calculating, objective investor would, without much hesitation at all, transfer his investment, would he not? Of course he would. Therefore, there must be reasons—other than prudence, cold, calculating and objective—that lead the owners to stand pat. Those reasons must be subjective, personal, preferential—they satisfy psychological needs. They define psychic income. Perhaps it is a belief that "If I hold on a little longer, things will get better." More often, at bottom, it is the presence of dismally unfavorable alternatives that leads the owners to keep the thing going.

So now we're ready to differentiate between "optimization" and "maximization." *"Optimization" deals with arriving at a blend of financial and psychic ROI such that the owners' expressed or perceived needs, wants, and preferences are met. Whereas "maximization" focuses exclusively on the financial ROI, and the goal is to make as high an ROI as practical, regardless of psychic income considerations.* Optimization strategies and tactics are more closely associated with Point B in Figure 1; whereas, maximization approaches and efforts are more commonly associated with Point A situations.

Up till now we've been reliant on accounting system data. And, by now, you know how flakey that can ofttimes be. Far too often we're forced to make management *and* ownership decisions based only on what the books say our assets are, what the books say our investment is. If we're really going to express the owners' demands in terms of ROI, it seems to me that THE most useful and revealing relationship between income and investment is, not surprisingly, based upon two non-accounting-system measures of investment. The most legitimate, valid, and accurate measure of the value of the shareholders' investment is *not* that which is defined by an accounting system devised and controlled by the owners. It is, rather, the value placed upon the company by professional outsiders in each of two situations. First, the net proceeds to the owners if the

firm were liquidated tells us the amount of *usable* or reinvestable funds available to the owners.

The second measure is the amount of usable, reinvestable
funds which would be available to the owners if the firm
were sold as an ongoing business. Regardless of what the
accounting system tells us about the value of the owners'
investment, these two measures tell us precisely how much
would be available as an alternate investment on which
some given rate of return would be achievable. And when
all is said and done, isn't that really the authentic, meaningful measure? Sure it is!

Suppose the firm's accounting system says that the financial ROI is 10 percent. So what? Standing in isolation,
that data point tells us nothing of any value whatsoever.
Having been told that the ROI is 10 percent, one still doesn't
have the foggiest idea whether to be overjoyed, pleased,
sad, or outraged. And until a person identifies where he
should be on the emotional spectrum, he will not know
what action to take. But suppose the owner is presented
with the following comparative array:

Accounting System:	10%
Liquidation:	14%
Sale of Firm:	12%

The owner can now analyze his real-world investment alternatives. Well, he can make 14 percent on liquidation, BUT
then he'd have nothing to do each day—he couldn't host
Christmas parties, he couldn't take those company-paid
off-shore trips with his wife, etc., etc. In other words, he
places a 4 percentage point value on psychic income; and,
at 4 percent, the optimal ROI is 14 percent (10 percent

financial ROI *plus* 4 percent psychic ROI) and thus exceeds the 12 percent obtainable on sale. The action strategy for this owner, in these circumstances and at this time, is both simple and rationally derived: stand pat; do nothing.

The best of all, however, is where the owner is able to sell and still remain in a chairman/CEO role! He is thus able to continue to enjoy the perks to which he's become accustomed *and* also be able to enjoy the improved, personal, financial ROI! In this case, his optimal ROI becomes 16 percent: 12 percent financial ROI on sale plus 4 percent psychic ROI.

Of course, one other factor must be accounted for when dealing with these two "real-world" measures of ROI. While ROI does express one relationship, the comparison of the successive or alternate denominators may not only be revealing but compelling as well. For instance, suppose the amount shown as investment by the accounting system is $1 million. Suppose further that liquidation will realize only $750,000, which is available then for reinvestment. Finally, let's say that the accounting system tells us that the financial ROI is 10 percent.

No owner is ever interested solely in "percent per share" (even if there were such a measure). Owners seek CASH first—and second and third, too, for that matter. And the more the better. Okay, then, with this in mind, let's examine the ROI picture presented in the hypothetical case above. An ROI of 10 percent says that the owner gets $100,000. If he is to get $100,000 from reinvestment of the liquidation proceeds, he must obtain a return rate of 13.3 percent. Not too hard to do really, as a passive investor. Then why not jump? Because the loss of psychic income occasioned by liquidation of the firm exceeds that amount which can be gained as only a passive investor with no perks, ego strokes, etc.

On the other hand, sale of the firm may realize capital appreciation. If the owner can obtain, say, $1.2 million for the firm, he need get only 8.3 percent to enjoy the $100,000 income stream. However, the balancing exercise occurs when the owner looks at $1.2 million at 13.3 percent! His income stream becomes $159,600 instead of only $100,000. Further, $26,600 of that amount is generated solely by the $200,000 premium from capital appreciation. Question: Does the psychic income enjoyed by the owner of the firm equal or exceed $59,600 per year? Only the owner can answer that, of course. But the additional income from the capital appreciation certainly tests the upper limit of the value of psychic income received.

RATIO MEASUREMENT AND CONTROL

As is readily seen, there are numerous ways to define and measure the owners' wants, needs, preferences, demands, and so forth. There is no single measure, unfortunately, that can adequately do the job. Nor is there a unique mix of measures that will do an adequate job in all cases. In other words, each firm, with its unique array and scatter of ownership, requires a tailored ratio measure mix. Listed below are sixteen of the more frequently used ratio measures. Try to use measures that can do double duty; choose measures that can both (a) define the owners' demands and (b) be used to track actual progress toward predetermined goals. In fancier terms, choose those measures that can be used for both planning and control.

A. *Current Ratio*
   Current Assets ÷ Current Liabilities
B. *Current Liabilities ÷ Net Worth*
C. *Total Liabilities ÷ Net Worth*
   This ratio measures the relative stake that creditors have in the business.
D. *Inventory ÷ Working Capital*
   Working Capital is defined as the *excess* of current assets over current liabilities.
E. *Accounts Receivable ÷ Working Capital*
F. *Long-Term Liabilities ÷ Working Capital*
   1. If the ratio value is greater than 100 percent, then proceeds of the long-term debt have most probably been diverted from working capital replenishment.
   2. The value of the ratio reveals how close the firm is to its long-term debt limit.
   3. This ratio measures the relative proportions that short- and long-term debt are of total Working Capital.
G. *Net Profit ÷ Net Worth*
H. *Net Profit ÷ Tangible Net Worth*
   Tangible Net Worth is the excess of assets over intangible assets minus liabilities.
I. *Net Sales ÷ Fixed Assets*
   This ratio is expressed in ''times'' rather than percent. It measures the adequacy (or lack thereof) of sales volume.

J. *Net Sales ÷ Working Capital*
Again, this measurement is expressed in "times" or turnover.

K. *Fixed Assets ÷ Net Worth*
This ratio measures the extent to which invested capital or net worth is tied up in nonliquid, permanent, depreciable assets. It reveals, too, the amount of net worth that is available for investment in liquid assets.

L. *Collection Period*
Commonly called "Days Sales Outstanding," or DSO, it is calculated in a two-step process. First, divide net sales by 365; then, divide that ratio *into* Total Trade Receivables.

M. *Net Sales ÷ Inventory*
This ratio is traditionally expressed in "turns." However, occasionally the ratio Cost of Goods Sold ÷ Inventory is also used to obtain additional insight into the "quality" of the turn ratio.

N. *Net Sales ÷ Net Worth*
Sometimes this is called the "trading" ratio. Usually, when the value of this ratio is very high, you will also find very large amounts of debt.

O. *Net Profit ÷ Net Sales*
Frankly, I prefer to use Operating Pre-Tax Profit ÷ Net Sales to more accurately discern the degree of "quality" of the profit generated by the ongoing, basic business.

P. *Miscellaneous Assets ÷ Net Worth*
Included in the numerator are: loans and/or advances due from officers, directors, and/or employees; prepaid

expense; deferred charges; other nonoperating investments; cash value of "key-man" life insurance; and
so on.

STEWARDSHIP

More often than you would otherwise expect, the owners
want their management to (merely) husband their assets;
just keep the dividends coming in—that sort of thing. The
obligation assumed by management is, to paraphrase the
presidential oath of office, "to preserve, protect and de-
fend" the dividend stream and balance sheet integrity.

This can be the most complex and challenging task that
operating management can ever face! You know the old
saw, "You either progress or regress—you cannot stand
still." Yet, in effect, that is exactly what the owners are
asking operating management to do. CAVEAT: Take on
this management assignment with great caution and circum-
spection. I was about to advise you to carefully evaluate
the downside risk, but that's a bit redundant—can a risk
ever be upside?

The biggest, most devastating risk that you face in this
type of assignment is technological obsolescence or strik-
ingly aggressive action by competitors. And it matters little
whether the firm's products/services are comprised of high-
tech or not. The higher the technological content, the greater
the jeopardy of being "out-tech'ed." And the closer the
resemblance to commodity-type products/services, the
greater the risk of profit performance erosion by, say, extreme price reduction action by the competition, either U.S.
or off-shore.

Some sage advice to owners who say they want to retain the status quo: You're far better off to pursue either Cash-In or Liquidate alternatives—take the proceeds and invest them in AAA muni's while you can still get an attractive amount of proceeds. Gather ye rosebuds while yet ye may and all that.

CASH IN: SELL THE FIRM

Okay, you've sweated, strained, and labored for twenty years or so and you've built up a really nice equity in your firm. But you know what? You've become *bored*. Yep, bored! Oh, some people call it burn-out or whatever. The point is, you no longer find it fun to go to the office every morning. Over the years you've taken your tax accountant's advice and took out less rather than more. Your son decided he wants to be an interior decorator and your daughter announced that she intends to take up residence full time in the condo you subsidized for her in Sausalito and try to find herself. So maybe it's time that you and your bride really got around to *doing* all those things you said you'd like to do. But how do you go about getting the *most* cash for your firm?

Unless you happen to be one of the very, very few who have had considerable and current (the laws do change, you know) merger and acquisition experience, the first thing you should do is shop for, select, and engage a "pro" to handle it for you. Continue to do that which you can do, that which put you in this enviable position in the first place—RUN YOUR BUSINESS! Hire a specialist to package, prepare, negotiate, and set up the closing for you.

After personal involvement (mostly as buyer for a big firm) in scores of sales of small- to midsized closely held firms, I can tell you that certain behavior patterns are virtually inescapable. You feel that you should handle it personally. After all, nobody know *your* business, your "baby," better than you, right? The bottom line is that you, the owner(s), are simply too emotionally involved to maximize sale proceeds. Every time you mention the word *I* at the negotiating table, you reduce the value of your firm by about $20,000! The last thing the potential buyer wants to hear is how crucially integral *you* are to the continued success of the firm. And that is just the first point I feel is important IF your objective is to Cash In. There are many, many more, but the following touch on significant, often overlooked, points.

1. *98 Percent of All Businesses Are Privately Held*
   Consequently, the vast majority of businesses which are sold are privately held. The buyer *can* afford to be choosy. He will have attractive alternate investment opportunities. At the outset, the buyer is not panting to buy your firm. You have some considerable selling to do IF you want to maximize sale proceeds.

2. *Owners Talk Too Much About the Past*
   Owners really enjoy spinning yarns for hours about how they started out just after World War II in the garage (substitute basement, substitute in-laws' garage, etc.). An owner will bend a buyer's ear for hours about how this plant was built, how that contract was negotiated, how that piece of equipment was selected, how

this piece of equipment was made right here when "Charley and I worked all night one Christmas Eve," and on and on.

All well and good, but the buyer couldn't care less! He's not buying the *past*—even if it's *your* treasured past! He wants to buy the *future*. And the more the owner talks about the past, the more he establishes Book Value as the initial ceiling price from which downward negotiating will begin. That will inescapably result in a price dramatically below that which a professional could obtain.

3. *Don't Value Your Firm Using "Multiple of Earnings"*
At best, this value is only an average. It cannot correctly present the unique value of your firm's future. There are much more relevant and legitimate methods of valuation.

Which "earnings" are you talking about? Are you talking about the earnings you reported for tax purposes? Or are you talking about the earnings you intentionally deferred or minimized?

4. *Price/Earnings Ratios Are a Meaningless Way to Value Your Firm*
In fact, use of P/E ratios for that purpose is forbidden in at least one state. In a privately held firm, sale of stock is so rare an event that determination of "Price," the numerator, is almost never quantified. As far as "Earnings," the denominator, is concerned, when was the last time you heard of a privately held firm run in such a way as to maximize taxes? That's what happens, of course, when you manage to maximize earnings.

5. *Sell Your Firm When the Market Is Ready—Even If You're Not!*

   Obvious? Sure, but you'd be surprised how many owners ignore that basic selling principle. Sometimes you just can't wait, I know. There may be health problems, estate problems, third-generation minority holders who want their cash, and so on. The point here is that IF you can exercise timing discretion, you will maximize proceeds by selling in a sellers' market. What are some of the key earmarks of a sellers' market? Well, among them are: low interest rates; the near-term prospect of low interest rates; high value of the U.S. dollar vis-à-vis other major free currencies; low inflation rate; and others, of course. Look for these conditions and circumstances that make it easy for the buyer to buy.

6. *Don't Begin the Sale Process Until You've Finalized Your Post-Sale Plan!*

   Wave the magic wand and lo! you have just been handed a certified check for $2 million more than you thought your firm was worth! Now what? The personal importance of the Post-Sale Plan to the seller is obvious. There's really no need to dwell on it. Still, a well-thought-out and documented Post-Sale Plan *will* add significant dollars to the proceeds of the sale. Why? Because the firm's value to the buyer increases as he is assured of an orderly transition, of the sellers' availability for a specific, even though brief, period. So, carefully documenting what it is you want/intend to do post-sale not only gives you and your family peace of mind, it will directly and substantially increase the gold for your Golden Years.

7. *The More Unique Your Firm's Market Niche, the More Attractive (that is, Valuable) You Are to a Big, Public Firm (With Lots of Money)*

Big firms ofttimes buy a small- to medium-sized firm as a way to learn about new markets and/or market segments. Big firms, by the way, usually pay more than another small entrepreneur would pay. For example, high and mighty Borg-Warner bought a small, privately owned travel agency in Colorado. Why did they do that? For two principal reasons. First, acquisition of an ongoing profitable firm is *really* a comparatively inexpensive way to learn about a new business. It's much more costly and takes far longer to bootstrap into a new, unfamiliar market.

Second, such an acquisition is often used as a prelude to a much larger scaled investment in that market/market segment. You can obtain an unusually high price if you're presented as the proper "toe-in-the-water." By the way, recent statistics show that about one of every three small firms who sold were bought by big firms.

Second "by the way." The importance and profitability of using a professional intermediary increases dramatically when the buyer is a big firm. Why? Because the buyers that are employed by a big firm couldn't care less about your personal history. They look, cold eyed, at numbers. I was there, and believe me, cutting deals is (can be) a highly impersonal affair. If this is the first time you have sold a firm (and more than 95 percent of the time that *is* the case) you are simply too emotionally involved. The hired guns of the buyer can easily and readily cut you, and your asking price, to pieces.

8. *Restate Your Historical Financial Statements*
Have your accountant rewrite your past *as if* your firm were run to maximize profit. Do *not* change the books of account! Just show the past in the same form that a potential big-firm buyer will quickly recognize and accept. The objective is to establish only the first element of your firm's value. Once you put back, for presentation purposes ONLY, all of the perk's and freebies, you will be surprised how much more profitable your firm was than perhaps even you thought. And how many times did you expense in the past even though they arguably could have been capitalized? And don't forget that you probably chose FIFO rather than LIFO!

9. *Prepare a Five-Year Business Plan*
The adage buyers never buy the past; sellers never sell the future! explains why more than four of every five firms are sold for less than the amount that could have been realized had a professional been in charge. Owners dwell on the importance and value of their efforts in the past—building up the firm, etc., etc. The buyer, on the other hand, wants to see reasonable likelihood of achieving a higher return on investment in the future by buying your firm rather than an alternate investment.

The more you know about the buyer's "hot buttons," the more closely can your Business/Profit Plan stress, highlight, and focus on them to your maximum benefit. The more highly the buyer prizes a "market niche" position, the more money you can get for your firm if you can convincingly present aggressive profit growth by exploitation of unique niche opportunities.

10. *Price = Terms = Price = Terms = . . .*
    Sight unseen, I hereby formally offer to buy your firm for $100 million! How's that for an offer? Want to take me up on it? Okay, let's set up a closing date for next week. By the way, I'll pay for your firm with $1 down and $1 per week. Hmmmm!

    The more definitely you document your Post-Sale Action Plan, the clearer will be your terms' requirements. They should be crystal clear in your mind *before* you even agree to sit down at the negotiating table.

11. *Foreign Firms Might (Usually Do) Pay More!*
    The relative political stability of the United States coupled with the strength of the U.S. dollar has led to the purchase of a considerable number of American firms by foreign acquirors. During the 1981–1985 period, some $53 billion, yes BILLION, was invested in America by foreign firms. That's the amount that foreign firms have paid to buy approximately 1,000 American companies.

    It's highly unlikely that the provincial owner will have effective entree to foreign firms and, consequently, higher sales prices. The value of a professionally connected intermediary can reap disproportionately large rewards for the astute, impersonal seller.

GROWTH

Too often, this owner objective is viewed almost as obligatory. That's unfortunate, really, because an awful lot of owners are truly not able to meet the personal and psychological demands that a *Growth* strategy requires. For our discussion, let's take the viewpoint of the new manager who is dealing with an owner who says he wants *Growth!* After all, that's all his pals at the club talk about, isn't it?

What do you do, Mr. Operating Manager? Well, the first thing you had better do is obtain a much closer and clearer picture and assessment of just how serious the owner is. If he talks about *Growth* in terms of new products, new markets, new facilities, new equipment, new people, and the like, you had better refer back to the section on *ROI,* because there's bound to be trouble in River City. Why? Because until the owner *starts out* with "income growth" or "wealth growth" as his prime objective, all he's talking about is spending cash, reducing income, and the like. The healthiest way to increase and sustain high levels of return on investment is by prudent *Growth!*

Test the owner's commitment and resolution. How does he *really* feel about:

1. Firing employees
2. Dropping product lines; individual products
3. Terminating distributors
4. Dropping unprofitable customers
5. Changing banks
6. Closing or selling plants and other facilities
7. Cutting or freezing fringes, perks
8. Reducing his own personal psychic income (very often THE most important!)

Of course, one way to find out is to ask him. But absent the demand to act, most people (owners included) wax nobly and freely. There must be a better way to plumb the depths of the owner's conviction. Of course there is. Merely examine the past and ascertain thereby what the owner has consistently *done* over time. It matters little what people say, they *always* reveal their emotions and feelings by what they *do*.

If you find that he has not managed in a No-Nonsense manner in the past, why should you believe that he really wants you to so manage now? Well, I would certainly be convinced if I learned that the creditors were putting pressure on the owner. And if he appeared genuinely perplexed about how to manage for *Growth,* I would tend to believe that he was serious. And if he promised not to play at being chief operating officer once he and I agreed on the quantitative *Growth* objectives, I'd take on the assignment.

LIQUIDATION

I intentionally left this alternative for last because, in my view, it is indeed the strategy of last resort. To get to this point, there must have been an irreversible, incurable breakdown of business management, planning, and control. There are now only two alternatives. Either liquidation was forced on the firm by the creditors, or the owner decided that the firm was worth more in liquidation than as a going business.

Neither of these alternatives is cheery—at least from an operating management point of view. In the final analysis, there are only growth problems or liquidation problems. It's been my experience that growth problems are ALWAYS better!

THE BOTTOM LINE

Owners/creditors ofttimes express their needs, wants, demands in prose and, more often, subjective, self-serving prose. They do so not because they are bad people, it's just easier for them to do it that way. Frequently, they speak in terms of "concern," "uneasiness," "worry," and so on. They generally use words like these because, on the one hand, they want to "go on record" with unhappiness and malaise, thereby establishing evidence of their business acumen. They want it to be known that they were astute enough to see the bad news developing. It puts them in position to utter, one more time, the ancient and revered staff-man mantra, "I told you so!"

On the other hand, they are usually incapable of defining or directing any specific, measurable action for which they could later be held accountable by the union, the employees, or, in some cases, the media. Quite often, they are not aware that they are incapable of operating management leadership. And these are the most "dangerous" of bosses (!) for they know not that they know not. Shun them; enter not into operating management employment contracts with them.

In sum, expect it to be very difficult to reduce the owners'/creditors' demands, etc., to numbers relatable to the Balance Sheet, Income Statement, and Cash Flow exhibits. Rarely, you will be happily surprised—but, alas! only rarely. If any meaningful progress is to be made, the task of reduction of demands of the owners to numbers is inescapable. Development of a run-rate forecast can usually be accomplished with facility. *But the "stretch" required of operating management can only be defined by subtracting the run-rate forecast from the Owners'/Creditors' demands. And it is* that *measured "stretch" which is precisely at the conceptual heart and core of incremental I gain.*

Absent measured "stretch," the definition of objective, measurable assignments or delegations is precluded. And without such professionally fashioned and chiseled assignments and delegations, effective monitoring of progress is only a futile hope. Not only are effective planning and control obviated, effective incentive compensation cannot be established or implemented. Thus, neither carrots nor sticks are available for our management kit-bag if we fail, first, to rigorously define the measured "stretch" between the run-rate forecast and the owners'/creditors' demands.

In Chapers 6 through 9 you will find specific, effective help in quantifying first the demands of the owners/creditors and second the measured "stretch" or operational performance gap between those demands and run-rate forecast.

Chapter 3

Operating Management—What Do They Really Do?

It's one thing to know or think we know what the owners/ creditors want, and quite another to achieve, perform, implement, obtain, and otherwise deliver to them what they say they want. We like to think that we know what operating management is all about. But if the truth were known, we know far less than we profess. Let's see if we can expand the boundaries of that knowledge. Let's start with "management" and then, later, sharpen our focus on "operating."

MANAGEMENT

The first thing an executive has to manage is himself. If he doesn't manage his own time, his own priorities, he won't have a chance to manage the company as he should. What is "management"?

> *Management is: getting work done through the efforts of others.*

That's simple enough. Or maybe it isn't, after all. Let's examine one word at a time. Consider "getting." Does this mean by persuasion? Or coercion? The first consideration deals heavily with style. Perhaps "getting" doesn't relate at all to style; perhaps its focus or central meaning is results. Nope, results seem more concerned with "work," which we'll get to in a moment.

Back to style or method. Shall we convince? Shall we motivate? A great deal more will be presented about motivation in Chapter 9. If the goal is to enhance the enduring value of the shareholders' investment (and that *is* the goal), the most effective style is to deal with people on a one-on-one basis. Recognize and deal with management and all employees as individuals. Why? Because people *are,* after all, individuals. Evaluate their performance on an individual basis. Reward their performance on an individual basis. Establish performance objectives on an individual basis.

By and large, most people want to do an outstanding job. They truly want to deliver an honest day's work for an honest day's pay. They want to feel important, to feel as though they do indeed have some meaningful say and control over their work and work environment. Most people truly want to be recognized, personally and by their peers and superiors, when their work honestly merits it. The effective manager takes resolute care to incorporate these principles in his management style. As Tryon Edwards once said, "He that resolves upon any great and good end has, by that very resolution, scaled the chief barrier to it."

Note the increasing reference to "work." What is "work"? Webster tells us that work is activity in which one exerts strength or faculties to do or perform something.'' He goes on, ''work may imply activity of the body [or] of mind.'' And, finally, ''it may apply to effort or to what is produced by that effort.'' Okay. *Any firm which is owned and/or managed by people who believe that ''work'' is synonymous with ''effort'' is either already bankrupt or very soon will be.* Owners and managers can learn a most important operating principle from—of all people—bankers! I have never heard, and I will give long odds that I never will hear, a banker ask about the level of or demand an improvement in ''effort per share.'' ONLY profit dollar/share counts! ONLY the *result* of effort matters and is of any interest.

Expend your effort, therefore, where you have the best chance for good return. As Robert Half, the CEO of a major executive recruiting firm, said, ''Success depends upon *doing* well what you can *do* well, and *not* doing what you *can't* do.'' Note the emphasis on ''Do.''

Let's continue with the definitional analysis, ''getting work *done*. . . .'' When, exactly, is work ''done''? The task of operating management is just like Mother's work: *It is never done.* While true as far as it goes, this answer is not useful because it doesn't go far enough. When should performance results be evaluated, judged? The answer to that question has two parts. First, the nature, scope, content, and substance of the assignment or task pretty much tells us when the results should be evaluated. For example, if the task or objective is to obtain $100 worth of new orders in September, then October 1 seems like a reasonable evaluation date. Oh, sure, we may want to pulse-beat how we're doing each week in September, but those are interim measures at best.

Second, we refer back to what the owners really want. If they want short-term, "fix-it-up-for-sale" action, then measurement in the short term is appropriate and the estimated sell price comparisons is the appropriate criterion.

How does the Incremental Gain concept provide the wherewithall to get the most done and done most effectively? It embodies the discipline that would have allowed Colonel Custer to defeat the entire Sioux Nation. He could have, you know, if he somehow could have gotten them to come over the hill one at a time. Incremental Gain Methodology explains why you should focus on one problem/opportunity, on one management task, on one performance objective at a time. And, as Josh Billings, a renowned humorist and author, instructs us, "Consider the postage stamp. It secures success through its ability to stick to one thing until it gets there."

Back to the mainstream. "Getting work done *through.* . . ." Amateurs and worse take this to mean merely manipulation. Professionals and practitioners of the Incremental Gains Methodology view this element, rather, as participative objective setting. It is recognition that no single manager can do it alone. Results, truly, are always the end product of a number of people. The central notion involved here closely parallels the notions discussed earlier in regard to the term "getting."

"Getting work done through the *efforts.* . . ." Once more we encounter the organizational motivational concepts that we discussed in "getting" and "through." This aspect, the motivation of the operating organization, is *so* important that it is presented in detail in Chapter 9. Note, though, that the reason why it is so important is because it magnifies the probability of successful *execution,* not of successful formulation of strategy. Thomas J. Watson, the founder of IBM, summed up one of the cardinal concepts, "Once an organization loses its spirit of pioneering and rests on its early work, its progress stops."

Finally, we get to, "getting work done through the efforts of *others*." Who, exactly, are the "others" through and with whom operating management seeks to achieve results? The first group that comes to mind is the operating organization itself: management, supervisors, and employees. The second group consists of both customers and vendors. The third group consists of the chief executive officer, the Board, the shareholders, the banks, the auditors, and the corporate legal counsel. Think of three concentric bands with the chief operating officer at the center. (Where else?) In-depth analysis and exploration of these intra- and interrelationships is a book by itself.

OPERATING MANAGEMENT

Having thus reviewed the highlights of what management is all about, let's focus more closely on operating management and the chief operating officer in particular, who, it would seem, is the linchpin of it all. An insight can be gained by thinking about some key elements of a Job Description for a chief operating officer. This will be useful because that description will (or should) be delegated throughout the operating organization. For openers, let's take a quick look at what is *not* included. Activities/duties which are not found include: "Develop corporate policy"; "Formulate strategy"; "Maintain favorable public and financial press relations''; ''Recommend and select the corporation's public accounting firm.'' Get the feel for what is *not* included in a chief operating officer's Job Description? Activities/duties which deal, essentially, with either (a) broad overview of the firm, or (b) ''external'' relations of the firm are, with only rare exception, the province of the chief executive officer, Mr. Outside.

The chief operating officer, then, is Mr. Inside. He does things, or is expected to do such things as: ''Prepare plans to achieve predetermined operational results''; ''Implement procedures consistent with and in furtherance of corporate policies''; ''Negotiate union labor contracts''; ''Prepare operational budgets to achieve minimally acceptable performance levels''; etc. He operates within the parameters established by the Board and shareholder approval of the chief executive officer's initiatives. Usually, the time horizon of the chief operating officer is much closer than that of the CEO. Also, usually, this does not mean that the chief operating officer is less farsighted than the chief executive officer. In fact, many times it is the case that the intimate familiarity with the workings of the corporate infrastructure enables the chief operating officer to actually be more effectively farsighted than the chief executive officer.

It's ''cute'' to point out that professional management means ''working *smart*'' not (merely) ''working *hard*.'' But no one that I know of ever went further to let us know how to distinguish ''working hard'' from ''working smart.'' You know, after some thirty years of bouncing around the business world, I'm not all that sure what ''working smart'' is. But I sure as hell have developed a feel for what "working hard" is all about. I've done more than my share of it. See if this doesn't ring a bell with you, too. Hard work is finally doing the accumulation of the easy things that you somehow didn't do when you should have!

A crucially important characteristic of operating management is that it is *line* management—management that is always "on the line" for generating the owners' desired results. The distinction between "line" and "staff" is both vital and not too easily drawn. An oft-cited difference is that the effectiveness of line management action is reflected, directly and virtually immediately, in the operating statements of the firm.

While that distinction is manifestly true, I believe that the essence of the difference lies much deeper, in the psyche. Regardless of the current job title held (many, many people become misassigned from time to time during their career) "line" and "staff" persons differ much more profoundly in the way they view the business world. That distinction is encapsulated in:

> *A line person strives to prove that something* can *be done!*
>
> *A staff person believes that proving that something* cannot *be done is equally important!*

THE NATURE AND RELEVANCE OF "CHANGE"

The central, fundamental characteristic which distinguishes the role of operating management from all others is the obligation to define, recommend, and, upon approval, effect *change* in the operating environment of the ongoing business. Yep, it's the mission of the operating management to keep the cutting edge of the firm sharp and well aimed. Operating management and change are two sides of the same coin. Charles F. Kettering, the principal management strategist of GM, said it: "The world may hate change, yet it is the only thing that has brought progress."

Since change is *so* fundamental and basic, it warrants some in-depth discussion. What are some of the important characteristics and insights related to "change"? *The* most important is that change is inevitable. That's right, inevitable. It *will* occur, in one form or another, whether you are the chief operating officer or not. From this moment forward, you shall not ever forget, *"And this too . . . shall pass!"* It will—and so will *you* and so will *I!*

Change is inevitable because the passage of time is inevitable. It's as simple as that. As part of nature, time passes with indifference for its consequences; with neither malice nor pity.

Further, if change is merely allowed to run its course, the result will always be unfavorable. In other words, if left to itself, the operating environment of the firm will deteriorate, will become less and less profitable. "Benign neglect" may be a useful political technique, but it won't get you anywhere in the marketplace if you're trying to make a profit.

Change, as it occurs, is virtually never perceptible. It almost never occurs in large doses: a missed order here; a late shipment there; an unenforced procedure; an incomplete product inspection; an unplanned personnel departure; and so on and so on. The amateur always succumbs to the temptation that no volitional, meaningful action is really needed—it will only upset everybody; things will get better next week, next month, next quarter. The economy will pick up. Geez! Can you imagine anyone relying solely on the whole U.S. economy to get his comparatively tiny firm better! Most every reader of this book operates in a minuscule portion of the economy. The economy could register, overall, a 10 percent improvement while the sliver that we serve plummets! And vice versa!

Change occurs incrementally. Remember, I'm talking about change in the operating environment of the firm. For example, while the ownership may change overnight, the operating environment—the plant, products, personnel, customers, vendors, and so on—has not changed. Perhaps even more important, changes always occur in small increments.

The corollaries are vitally important to a full understanding of the nature of operating management. Change can occur *only* in small increments. And change in human behavior, if it can occur at all, occurs in yet even smaller increments. No surprise, really. Haven't you heard for years and years that people resist change?

The consequence of these corollaries is that the likelihood of success of management action plans is inversely related to the magnitude of the planned change. That is, the smaller the planned change, the more likely it is that it will be successfully implemented. But much more of this concept and its attendant inferences and consequences in Chapter 4.

The rate at which change occurs also varies. In general,

unfavorable changes occur faster and more frequently than do favorable changes. They occur more frequently because there are more unfavorable forces at work at any one time than there are favorable ones. They occur faster because they require only inaction, inattention, and inadvertance to make them happen.

Yet even favorable changes occur at varying speeds. The rule is, the less the change sought is people-related, the faster can be its implementation. It is very easy to buy or sell a machine, put up some warehouse shelving, or change a price list that is already on a computer. However, it is very difficult to obtain acceptance of accountability by someone who has never before been so held.

There can be no progress or growth without change! That is not to say, of course, that all change yields progress or growth. Mindless, purposeless management-by-thrashabout generates many, many changes and absolutely no progress. If the owners/creditors want improved financial return, increased earnings, and a higher value on their investment, the operating management is expected and obligated to prepare conforming and supportive plans for change.

The twin obligation exists to inform and advise the owners/creditors of the likelihood of achieving alternate goals/objectives. In other words, if the wants of the owners/creditors exceed the grasp of the operating management, then they must simply be made aware of the practical performance maximum that can be realistically achieved. Once operating management accepts the obligation to deliver performance at a given level within a given time, it becomes accountable and responsible for progress and results.

Because the notion of growth connotes performance levels higher, or more favorable, than those previously attained, operating management must somehow see to it that operating personnel perform at somewhat higher, more productive levels than those previously attained. Simply put, *it's "Star Trek" time!* We must (boldly) go where the firm has not been before.

Uncertainties abound and lie quietly in wait as we embark on our quest. Not only are we really not sure if our personnel will be able to measurably improve performance, we face exogenous variables—that is, we face impact from vagaries of circumstances and events external to and uncontrollable by our firm.

To some tangible extent, the likelihood of achieving the performance objectives to which we are committed are affected by those external factors. Sometimes serendipity occurs, but more frequently the effect is unfavorable. What are some of these external factors? Not necessarily ranked in severity of impact, the following discusses many of them.

You are dependent on your customers. And if your firm is like every firm that I have ever worked with for more than twenty-five years, less than 20 percent of the accounts generate more than 80 percent of your volume. The greater the "repeat" or "post-delivery" order volume, the greater is your dependency upon them as a source of continuing volume. The larger the percentage share that each customer buys of the total sales volume, the more difficult it will be to increase sales to that customer. Further, the more difficult it will be to increase sales by raising prices.

Customers can, of course, be lost for reasons other than the failure to properly serve and service them. For example, a customer may be acquired by another firm whose policies or practices preclude continuance. But this doesn't happen all that often because the general rule is that if the customer finds a relationship to be profitable to him, he will continue it. And the most prevalent criterion is that you supply the answer to his problem at less cost than any known alternative.

There are other factors, of course. The customer has filed for Chapter 11. If you were doing even a mediocre management job, you should have foreseen this development. But foresight, alone, does *not* replace the volume. You certainly should have had enough early warning to avoid serious bad debt exposure.

Your customer's business is doing just fine. But the product for which you supply parts is discovered to be unprofitable and so it has been dropped from *his* product line. Or, the product was redesigned for cost reduction and your components were designed out. Or, they substituted a different material for yours.

And it is increasingly more the case that many firms are finding it more profitable to switch to products made outside of the U.S.: Mexico, Taiwan, Hong Kong, Korea, and the Philippines seem to be the most popular. Unless your firm has operational facilities in these areas, you will have lost the volume.

Suppose your business enjoys high-margin, post-sale parts volume. Your customer decides to make the parts himself. Or a new, low-cost, low-overhead competitor enters the market and low-balls the price. In summary, there are many, many marketplace vagaries which may eventually impinge on prior and present sales volume.

Many factors beyond your control can also affect your vendors. Again, the first alternative is that the vendor becomes bankrupt. Clearly, your jeopardy increases as the technological or special purpose content of the purchased item increases. Sure, a common defense is to qualify several vendors. Okay, but where do you draw the line—especially when there is costly tooling involved? When does the additional cost of purchasing exceed the potential gain of reduction in purchasing cost?

The vendor, on the other hand, let's suppose, is very successful and grows rapidly. The value to him of your business drops month by month and year by year. Delivery becomes more uncertain and, would you believe, you're beginning to notice some quality problems that you never encountered before. And the vendor is not only raising price by more than anticipated, he's tightening up pay terms, too. Your Cash Flow Plan gets deeper and deeper into trouble.

What's the bottom line of all of this? Well, first of all, reaching new, higher levels of performance is not easy, even if all goes reasonably well, but particularly so if there is an element of ''stretch'' in the performance objectives. Second, ''change'' itself generates stress and anxiety within your operational organization that exacerbates the unlikelihood of achieving the objectives which you are obligated to attain. Third, the changes in developments and events outside the firm usually further impede and otherwise heighten obstacles in your path to progress.

To sum up: *''Vulnerability'' is the hallmark, the fundamental feature, the psychic cornerstone of operational management.* If you haven't learned to be comfortable while you're vulnerable, you cannot be a successful operations manager.

How do you gain comfort while being vulnerable to forces beyond your control: By practicing Monday-morning quarterbacking? By changing the demands by the owners, the Board, the chief executive officer? To coin a phrase, it ain't easy! But some sources of solace are readily available. Take heart! First of all, be aware that there are a whole lot of operational guys out there facing the same things you are. If misery loves company, rest assured in the knowledge that you are definitely not alone.

Recognize that the evaluation of your performance really rests on your "batting average." To give you a little perspective, Babe Ruth, in his lifetime, hit 714 home runs. And *that* is what he's known for! That is what kept his name in the record books for decades. You have to dig a little deeper in that same record book to discover that he struck out 1,330 times! Yep, that's right! He struck out almost twice as often as he hit a home run. But who cares?

EXECUTION

Okay, so much for solace. Let's move to a little tougher stance. To succeed at anything is never easy. If it were, the value of that success would be trivial. As a matter of fact, the more difficult the challenge, the harder it is to capture success, the sweeter, the more rewarding, the more valuable the success.

To be a successful operations manager, failure must be anathema; a hateful, shameful thing. Failure costs you something—personally. It can cost you financially: a blown bonus; a passed-over promotion; a postponed salary raise; even employment termination. On the other hand, success demands a price. And the greater the success, the higher the price. Bottom line: *It is always better to pay the price of success than to suffer the cost of failure.*

Only 3 percent of all people are "winners." And even they fail about 49 percent of the time at what they try to do. So why then are they winners? They are successful; they are winners because they actually do accomplish, achieve, finish many more things with 51 percent of their time than the other 97 percent of the people do with 100 percent of their time.

"Secrets" about achieving success? Well, maybe not secrets, but a couple of insights might be helpful. *"Follow through" is immeasurably more important than "initiation."* It's easy as hell, nowadays, to launch a passenger-carrying space ship. But bringing it back home safely and on time with its mission fulfilled? Well, that's the tough part. So while the Board, the chief executive officer, or some crisp eagle-eyed staffer may "initiate," it's the operations manager and his organization who must "do," who must execute. Almost anyone can "conceptualize," but only a rare few can "get it done," can execute, can follow through.

How many times have you heard the futile excuse for unacceptable performance that goes something like, "I had *so* many fires to put out." What that ineffective manager is really saying is that he failed to prioritize the firm's problems/opportunities so they could be confronted one at a time, in sequence of descending importance.

Oh, sure, easy to say, huh? Just how do you really do it? How in the hell do you identify the priority of the problems and opportunities? Well, there *is* one approach that I've used over the years, and it seems to have successfully stood the test of time. You start by getting a bunch of index cards. Then, in conjunction with the owners, the creditors, key customers, key vendors, organizational functional heads, and other key operating personnel, you write a description of the problem/opportunity as quantitatively as possible—ONE TO A CARD.

As the cards are completed, route them to the chief financial officer or comptroller with the assignment to record on each and every card the current year estimated impact on operating profit. Approximation is desired; time wasted by pursuit of pointless precision only compounds the problems and delays exploitation of the opportunities.

Next, sort the cards in descending sequence by operating profit impact. Review the roster with the owners to make sure you attack first what *they* want attacked first. Then, at a Management Action Meeting with your appropriate (that is, cognizant) personnel, complete assignment delegation of *only* the top ten. And if you forget this entire book, do NOT ever forget that only some meetings achieve length while all of the others have length thrust upon them! In one to two weeks, convene yet another meeting with the owners to reconfirm the priority action sequence; then meet again with the responsible subordinates, assess and record progress—*task by task*—and assign the responsibility for the next five. And so on, and so on.

In this way the owners are assured that action *is* occurring and that the action occurring is the action they want taken.

The focus of your key personnel is kept solidly on those projects that have the greatest operating profit impact, and they are beginning to get a taste of achievement as well as being held accountable for measurable results. Finally, the key customers and vendors as well as the employees, almost without exception, react extremely well to be given the chance to participate.

So far so good. Now, suppose we're working on a project which has, say, an estimated operating profit impact of $100,000, and let's also say that it heads our current top-ten list. The managers responsible for problem resolution/ opportunity exploitation tell you, "We can get some $90,000 to $95,000 in about three weeks. It will probably take another month or two to get the other $5,000 to $10,000." What do you tell them to do? Well, I would tell them to go for the $90,000 to $95,000, see if they can get it in less than three weeks, and *close the project!* REMEMBER: Self-confidence (or motivation) is ALWAYS a product of action, never a product of (only) planning! Reassign the remaining $5,000 to $10,000 impact to where it would normally fall in the descending sequence and treat it accordingly. That approach illustrates the pivotal difference between being *effective* and being (only) *efficient*. There is another way to illustrate the difference. And chances are, you'll probably remember this longer:

> *Always put off until tomorrow the things you shouldn't do today anyway!*

We do, in fact, live and manage in a 95 percent world. No, I wouldn't go so far as to be pleased with half a loaf because of the adage, "half a loaf is better than no loaf."

I do not go that far because half a loaf is, after all, *only,* half of a loaf! But 95 percent of a loaf is damn near a *whole* loaf! I'll take that! From an operational management viewpoint, do not ever expect, really, to get the *very* last drop! I guess, in the entire universe, there is only one case where you *can* expect it—and that is only a brand of coffee.

Hand in hand with the imperative to never settle for mediocrity is the inferential imperative to never delay enacting personnel decisions, especially terminations. In other words, when someone simply fails to perform, it's time for you to remember that you are not obligated to magically transform that individual into a winner. Remember what I said about "effort per share"? Well, it goes double for "personnel-salvages per share." Namely, if we take this crusading spirit to the extreme, we will wind up with a bunch of improved rehabs just at the time that the locks and chains are fastened to the front gate.

How can you tell the winners from the losers? There are a number of tests. Among those that I've found the best are:

A winner always has *an* answer.
A loser is always part of the problem.

A winner always has a program.
A loser always has an excuse.

A winner sees answers for *every* problem.
A loser sees problems in *every* answer.

A winner says it might be difficult, but it is possible.
A loser says it might be possible, but it's too difficult.

The sad truth is that people simply cannot change once they've reached an age of "adulthood" in a business environment. Might as well face up to it. Again, yet again, unless the owners specifically direct you otherwise, quickly remove those who impede.

Why this sense of urgency? Most simply because until the shirkers, the losers, the subperformers are removed, time will not be on the side of the owners. And what does that mean, "Time is on your side"? In a nutshell, it means "Because of all the actions you took or will take today, the operating conditions of your firm will almost certainly be better tomorrow." It means things are going your way.

If an operating manager is self-confident, strongly motivated, and capable of excellent results, he cannot be *so* amateurish as to look at the world through rose-colored glasses. Yet be mindful that excellence never proceeds from looking at a rose through world-colored glasses! *L'adace! Toujours l'adace!* Bold never means careless.

One of the most cogent, useful summaries of the essence of operating management that I have ever seen appeared in the *Wall Street Journal* on November 26, 1984, in an article entitled "Manager's Journal" by M. Feinberg and A. Levestein. They reduced the awesome task of getting your operations personnel to act with a "go-go" spirit to only six "commandments." They may just have gotten it all on only one stone tablet!

Nevertheless, I'm obligated to share their "expertise" with you. They're not really all that bad, after all (nor are they all that awesomely profound that they're arcane).

1. "Show a personal interest in individual progress." I believe that if the progress is impersonally measured, it means *much* more!
2. "Build charismatic relationships." Well, those are, after all, the best kind, *n'est pas?*
3. "Encourage others to shine." (Note: If you're the chief operating officer, then getting the chief executive officer to shine—particularly if he's also the controlling owner—won't hurt!)
4. "Provide psychological support." (*But* only if the owners say that it's okay to spend their money that way.)
5. "Ask questions, but in a special way." The idea is to stimulate new options. If a chief operating officer is anything, he *must* be a burr under the bureaucracy's saddle!
6. "Keep people informed." That's the *most* important of these six! Really it is. If anyone, at anytime, gets the notion that information is being withheld, then everything starts to deteriorate.

Chapter 4

Management by Incremental Gains

Okay, so perhaps Voltaire never did run a company! Nevertheless, he speaks to us "line guys" from across a couple of centuries. And what he said then makes startlingly good sense today: "Perfection is attained by small degrees."

In Chapter 3, we talked about management—operating management. We discussed its nature and purpose. In this chapter we start off by establishing the criterion by which the effectiveness, or "goodness," of line operating management should be measured. Luckily, the criterion can also be simply stated:

> *Effective management is that management which enhances the enduring value of the shareholders' investment.*

Further, the greater the degree or amount of enhancement, the better. There is no cap or ceiling. Owners can never be (or become) too wealthy. This characteristic is at once the source of all things noble, and all things vexing and mischievious about the profession of management. All things noble because those who are truly inspired unrelentingly pursue their quest for excellence. All things vexing because of the unceasing frustration of never being able to fulfill the quest for excellence. All things mischievious because the constant state of imperfection provides continually fertile ground in which the Monday-morning quarterbacks thrive and fluorish.

The only thing that affects the enduring value of the shareholders' investment is what gets *done,* what gets recorded in the financial records of the firm. When the swirling dust of frenzied effort, heated debate, and behind-the-back politicking finally settles, it is the FACTS of *Change* and the irreversible events that ultimately determine what, if anything, has happened to the enduring value of the shareholders' investment.

Events will occur. Change will alter operating circumstances. The enduring value of the shareholders' investment will be altered. The challenge to you and me—the professional manager—is to sufficiently anticipate the likely consequences so as to arrange affairs to produce favorable events, change, and alterations of the enduring value of the shareholders' investment. How can we tell whether the manager is doing a good job or not? There are only two criteria that provide relevant, meaningful comparisons to actual performance. The first is the COST incurred by the implementation action, the execution, the *doing.* The second criterion is the length of TIME that it took to complete that action. Of course, the less of each that is expended, the better.

In a way, these two criteria are interchangeable. Someone once said, "Time is money." So, therefore, if a given level of results can be achieved with less cost and/or time than originally thought or planned or actually incurred previously, the more effective is the management. Note that both of these criteria are measurable, objective, impersonal, and quantifiable. Note further that the data needed to measure the cost criterion lie generally within the accounting system; while measurement data for the other criterion, time, lie external to the firm's accounting system. The time measurement is not only the more reliable one, it is also the more important one! If a given result is desirable at all, then it must be more desirable the sooner it is achieved or realized, according to the law of time value of gratification. Resources of all types are deployed, redeployed, or dedicated to achieving a given objective result. If those resources were not so dedicated, they could be employed in other pursuits, or they could be dispensed with, along with their support costs. In other words, the longer it takes to achieve a given result, the longer limited resources are tied up, the higher the opportunity cost that is incurred.

ACCOUNTABILITY

This is a crucial concept. Because it is so often only partially understood or misunderstood, it is best to take a little time here to make sure we're both on the same page of the hymnal.

At bottom, being accountable connotes recognition of an obligation to perform in a predetermined manner. Both performance of an action(s) and forebearance of performance of an action(s) are included within the concept. Is it possible to be accountable and not recognize that the obligations exist? Yes, of course. But it is extremely rare that such a condition exists at top levels of business management, so we won't waste any time exploring the inferences and consequences.

The heart or essence of the task of management is to hold others accountable. The mere presence of a sense of accountability announces the existence of a superior-subordinate relationship. The burden rests with the superior to ensure that the subordinate does indeed (a) recognize that the accountability obligations exist, and (b) performs in a manner such that the recognized accountability obligations are satisfactorily fulfilled, met, or otherwise discharged.

The superior strives to hold subordinates accountable. The difficulty of that task is mitigated if the subordinate either inherently possesses a sense of accountability (responsibility) or can be taught to be accountable. Ancient wisdom tells us that the most effective way to make someone trustworthy is, simply, to trust him. Applying that principle to this situation, the most effective way to instill (or enhance) accountability is to implement an incentive compensation program which (a) allows the participant to measure his own progress and resulting reward as he strives to meet/exceed quantitative performance objectives, and (b) publicizes each participant's progress (or lack thereof) to all fellow participants in the program.

For accountability to exist, there must be an auditable standard or measure against which comparisons to actual performance can be made. A truly important principle is that the more quantitative the measure to which the subordinate can be held accountable, the more likely, the easier it is that the measure or standard will be met. The easier it is for the subordinate to personally ascertain where he stands, the more effective is the communication and the less prevalent is the practice of "office politics." REMEMBER: If your objective is (it never should be) to intimidate and frustrate subordinates, use ONLY qualitative measures of performance, of results. A measure, for instance, which says, in part, "Run the operation effectively," is just the right language to keep a subordinate perpetually off balance. "Handle the major accounts appropriately" is another example of the type of accountability measure used by insecure amateurs.

Finally, steps and techniques that should be used to hold subordinates accountable are discussed in considerable detail in my earlier book, *No-Nonsense Planning* (The Free Press, 1984). Let's see if we can capture most of the highlights here. First of all, the keystone upon which all else is based is your subordinate's perception of you as the dispenser of both his rewards and punishments. That's tantamount, of course, to exercising power over someone. But it is impossible to exercise power over someone who does not feel vulnerable, whether he really is or not.

Establishing vulnerability is a three-step process. First, give someone an assignment. Second, enforce the obligation to "explain." It is essential to establishing vulnerability that the subordinate must recognize his personal obligation to explain (in a Manager's Monthly, or Weekly, Report, no less) that for which he is being held accountable.

The "obligation to explain" is a powerful psychological force. And when the subject of the explanation is a numbers-variance (for example, booked orders were only $80 and the objective was $100), the further burden of explaining what *additionally* must be done to *recoup* the shortfall is usually even more serious. In effectively managed firms, this force is consistently marshaled on behalf of the shareholders.

There are only three types of management. Most firms are run by amateur management. Not stupid management, mind you, but merely management ignorant of professional principles and practices—incompetent, lacking the qualities (skills, talents) necessary to effect independent action. The second largest group of people who manage businesses comprise what I would term "pseudo-professional." That is, they are aware (perhaps mostly vaguely) of and do (most often partially) practice many professional management principles. They will, for example, enforce the obligation to explain upon subordinates. But they customarily use *only* the stick, and almost never use the carrot (except, of course, for themselves and their cronies on the Board or in officer positions). This type of management consistently generates heat but absolutely no light at all, lots of stress but no strength!

The third group, rare in number, are truly professionally managed firms. They, of course, use the stick when required, but—and this is crucially important—they also generously use the carrot. Yes, objectives are quantitative, independently measurable, and impersonal. Yes, the obligation to explain variances of actual results is, indeed, enforced. However, the objectives are established at a "stretch" level such that extra effort, extra work, extra action must be expended to meet or exceed them. NOW the CARROT!

An *open-ended* Incentive Compensation Program provides uniquely attractive opportunities to earn truly interest-
ing and motivating sums of money. Thus, the pressure to
achieve the objectives is generated by the employee himself
(and his wife if you inform her of the program) and not,
repeat NOT, solely by the superior! And therein lies the
distinguishing characteristic which separates the pseudo-
professional from the true professional.

The lesson? When you have devised an array of financial
objectives such that (a) they are personally assignable so
that individuals can be held accountable, have the obligation
to explain, and (b) they will significantly and importantly
enhance the enduring value of the shareholder investment,
(c) they can be reliably and independently measured, and
(d) there is no limit on the amount of incentive compensation that the participant can earn as he reaches and exceeds
his objectives—then, my friend, you will already have led;
you are ready to follow, and you will have demonstrated
the managerial courage to "get the hell out of the way"
of the tigers that you have bred.

Returning to the mainstream, the third step in the process
of establishing vulnerability as part of management's Incentive Compensation Program is to expose the participant's
actual performance compared to the performance objectives
to which he was earlier committed.

Of primary importance is the fact that emphasis placed
on the increments of improvement, per se, forces management focus on OPPORTUNITIES FOR PROFIT, and not
on the problems that stand in the way of making profit!
Increased owner wealth must eventuate as the focus of
operating management centers on ways to exploit opportuni-

ties to increase profit rather than to merely find solutions to apparent or surface problems. Thus, at the same time, and with the same management reporting and control system, it is possible to positively appeal to the full array of employees—from those who aspire to practice elements (at least) of entrepreneurship to those who perform best with merely technocratic or bureaucratic challenges.

THE NINE POSTULATES OF MANAGING BY INCREMENTAL GAINS

Listed below are the nine postulates, principal presuppositions, and/or premises which comprise the framework of the concept of incremental gain. They are listed in no particular priority or sequence. They are, however, largely interdependent.

Postulate No.1: The Effectiveness of Management Increases in Proportion to Increases in Effectiveness of Accountability

Recall that Effective Management was defined earlier as that which enhances the enduring value of the shareholders' investment. Thus, this postulate really says that the better the practice of accountability, the greater the enhancement of the enduring value of the shareholders' investment. And the practice of accountability is a twin-effort.

First must be Job Description, Performance Evaluation, and Incentive Compensation Programs such that the subordinate can easily understand and measure what is expected of him and can reliably measure his progress toward those obligations. It is in this manner that excuses for lack of accountability are precluded to subordinate use. Thus, the subordinate must (a) understand what his performance obligations are and (b) be motivated to strive to meet/exceed those obligations.

Second, management must meet its obligation to hold subordinates accountable. There are, in turn, two aspects to this obligation. One is, essentially, an intellectual challenge heavy with the burden of anticipation and foresight. Management must measure the future and calibrate the component work elements. Management must plan. Management must anticipate time intervals and resource investments required to overcome the obstacles that stand in the way of meeting objectives.

The other aspect is the largely unpleasant task of performing the role of the shareholders' conscience. Management must regularly, periodically, and publicly (that is, in the presence of peers and subordinates whether that presence takes the form of physical presence or distribution of written reports) inquire as to the results achieved to date (status) and to the outlook for task completion (prognosis). Management must ask, almost in a parental manner, "You promised to mow the lawn by noon. It is now 1:00 P.M. Did you mow the lawn or not?" Such well-defined tasks and questions ("You were to obtain $100 in new orders for Product A at no less than 38 percent gross margin by September 16. How much was actually booked?") tend to make people uncomfortable. If the task is not well defined, then the superior feels uncomfortable because he has no way to avoid a "snow job" by a failing subordinate. On the other hand, if the task *is* well defined, the subordinate tends to feel uncomfortable, particularly if he didn't mow the lawn within the time promised. But even if he did, there will come a time when he will not and the burden of explanation will become awesome, indeed.

All things otherwise equal, however, the shareholders are unquestionably far better off if the subordinates are uncomfortable rather than the superiors.

Postulate No. 2: The Effectiveness of Accountability Increases as the Number of Intermediate Work Steps Decreases

No surprise here. Pretty straightforward, really. Common sense tells us that it is easier both to be accountable and to hold others accountable if there are fewer results or events to keep track of rather than more.

There is another aspect that warrants attention. Let's suppose that one of the objectives of the vice president sales is to increase annual margin by $100 through price increase action. If the objective is defined in, say, October, and the fiscal year is the calendar year, then some fourteen months must elapse before we shall know whether or to what extent the objective was achieved. Not only will the subordinate have escaped accountability, the shareholders will have been disserved. Mind you, this is *not* the fault or blame of the subordinate! It is, rather, the fault of top-level management for not having properly defined the objective in the first place.

The solution? You're probably way ahead of me. Set

up the annual objective, of course, but show it as the cumulative effect of quarterly objectives, or even monthly objectives. For instance, a monthly objective could be shown in two parts: (1) the increase percent and amount to take effect that month, and (b) the year-to-date cumulative effect of price increase action. Much better, eh? Sure!

Remember, price increase action is particularly nourishing for the firm. Dollar for dollar, it falls, undiminished, all the way down to the operating pre-tax line. Generally, this action is as precious as expense reduction, *not* cost reduction.* There is a strong, meaningful distinction between these two avenues of approach.

There is, of course, no magic number of intermediate work steps which is guaranteed to generate optimal results. The principal variables are, first, the nature (scope, size, complexity, duration, etc.) of the objectives, and second, the individual who is responsible and accountable for its achievement.

Interestingly enough, it seems that a rough, yet workable guideline in a range of six to twelve intermediate steps generally works out pretty good.

Postulate No. 3: The Effectiveness of Accountability Increases as the Number of Annual Objectives Increases to Optimal Levels

Traditional wisdom along the rock-bound coast of Maine tells us that it is far easier to catch a whale with 1,000 small hooks than it is with only one, very large hook.

---

* See my earlier book, <u>THE</u> *Turnaround Manager's Handbook,* The Free Press, 1985, for explanatory details.

There is, of course, a practical limit on the number of objectives that can either be assigned or monitored effectively. Too many tasks or objectives means that no one of them will receive the attention that is necessary for successful achievement. On the other hand, if there are too few objectives, the greater the jeopardy of performance failure for two reasons. First, there might be an inadequate number of objectives to achieve the shareholders' desired overall result. Second, failure to meet one or two of only a few objectives most probably would result in failure to earn any incentive compensation. If that were to happen, interest in and commitment to achievement of any remaining objectives will probably falter. Morale of the management corps could most likely plummet, causing even more serious performance shortfalls.

Again, the range of the number of objectives that seems to obtain the best results in the real world is six to twelve. Not too many to cause inabililty to perform by the responsible person and not too few so that failure to achieve one or two does not completely preclude earning at least some incentive compensation.

Postulate No. 4: Difficulty of Implementation Decreases as the Size of the Work Unit or Task Decreases

It's a great deal easier to perform a relatively simple task than it is to complete a complex piece of work. A corollary holds that the longer it takes to complete an assignment, the less likely it is that it will be successfully performed. Remember what Voltaire said about "small degrees"?

Makes excellent common sense, doesn't it? Sure it does. Forget fancy management theories. It makes down-home common sense that the less you're expected to do, the more likely it is that it will get done. It is *always* easier to perform a small, simple task than it is to perform a lengthy, complex one. The converse, then, is obvious. Namely, define performance objectives only in such a manner that they are easily measurable. To the extent that you are successful will be the measure of the magnitude and complexity of the assignment that you make.

Postulate No. 5: Effectiveness of Communication Increases as the Magnitude of the Task Decreases

Common sense tells us that the shorter the message, the more likely it will be transmitted accurately. Therefore, the smaller, the simpler the assigned task, the more likely it is that effective, complete communication will be successfully achieved. After all, recall that an inch is, indeed, a cinch, and a yard is, indeed, very hard.

Postulate No. 6: Reliance on Automated Reporting Systems Diminishes as the Number of Tasks Assigned, or Numbers of Objectives Committed to Diminish

This is a highly important concept for several reasons. Among them are, first, it usually takes more time, cost, and effort to install an automated reporting system than it does to install a manual system. Second, while an automated reporting system, once installed, can indeed process numerous transactions at a much lower unit cost compared to a manual system, it is usually much more costly to make changes in the work unit content description and/or performance criteria than manual edits of a lesser number of work units.

The virtue of simplicity is confirmed yet once again. Less cost is incurred, more flexibility is provided, communication is personalized, and prompt initiation is enhanced. Therefore, the likelihood of successful execution is profoundly promoted.

Postulate No. 7: Ease of Implementing an Effective Reporting System Increases as Dependence on Accounting System Data Decreases

The notion of "effective" reporting embodies several features. First and foremost, it should mean a reporting system which is accepted by the accountees as representing results and comparisons in a fair, unbiased, and duplicable manner. It is far too widely known that accounting system data are prone to subjective, judgmental vagaries. Despite the existence of "generally accepted principles," there are many opportunities for management and/or owners to portray actual results in varying hues from black to red and vice versa. Consequently, those who are held accountable for results would much prefer to be measured by yardsticks which they, themselves, can apply independently to the data. Number of pounds shipped, for example, is much preferred as a measure of performance than margin dollar content of shipments. Similarly, number of full-time employees is preferable to gross payroll "costs."

"Effectiveness" also includes the idea of control. That is, the more the accountee feels that his performance is judged on activities over which he can personally exercise control, the greater will be his understanding of both his commitment and his progress toward that objective. As his understanding increases, so also does his motivation and, thereby, also the likelihood of successful execution.

Further, there is value in learning sooner of actual-to-standard comparisons of performance rather than later. A favorite No-Nonsense adage is, *"The shorter the control cycle time, the more effective the control."* Performance comparison data which must come from the accounting system cannot, usually, be available for management reporting and control purposes until after the books have been closed. So the prudent and effective general manager will maximize use of accounting-system data (to the extent it is otherwise unavoidable), which can be gleaned as early in the monthly closing cycle as possible. Nonetheless, non-accounting-system data are always available quicker than accounting-system data.

Postulate No. 8: Integrity of the Incentive Compensation Program Increases as the Size of the Unit of Work or Tasks Decreases

What do I mean by "integrity"? Well, included are a number of characteristics. Among the important ones—those which enhance the likelihood of successfully achieving/exceeding the performance objectives—are: fairness; clarity; independent audit; understanding; ease of measurement (that is, objective rather than subjective); timely; complete; and simple, open, and uncomplicated administration and publication.

It is, of course, crucial to achievement of "stretch" objectives that the Incentive Compensation Program does indeed provide concrete, positive motivation. In far too many mismanaged firms, the so-called Incentive Compensation Program installed by amateur (to be kind) management become, themselves, obstacles—potholes, if you will—in the path performance achievement.

The smaller the unit task, the simpler it can be stated and measured, the more easily it can be understood, independently audited, and so on. Smaller and simpler task descriptions lend themselves directly, then, to enhancement of the integrity of the Incentive Compensation Program and, thereby, to enhancement of prospects for successfully achieving performance objectives.

Postulate No. 9: Likelihood of Approval of a Profit Plan, Product Plan, or Budget Increases as the Size and Complexity of the Unit Tasks Decrease

The basic underlying reason for the veracity of this postulate is the truism that the easier it is to understand something, the sooner it will be accepted, absorbed, and (even) endorsed. An intriguing and captivating lesson we learn from successful negotiations is, that when we get the "fellow across the table," our adversary, to nod quickly and frequently in approval, success is within our grasp. And the way we initiate that nodding approval phenomenon is to present notions, concepts, ideas in small enough doses that they are appealing, appetizing, and, most importantly, easily digestible and assimilable.

Once you start eating peanuts you can't stop, right? Ever hear of that? Ever experience that? You "know" it's true! Once you start you could eat a pound of 'em, couldn't you? Sure! BUT! Suppose you were presented with a single, huge, one-pound peanut? Can you imagine? Chances are you'd refuse to even start on it. More about the application of these postulates in Chapter 5.

If you're with me thus far, I'm sure you'll continue. It is a short jump from sustained favorable nodding to signed-off approval. When you sit there for hours saying, "Yes, yes," with nods, there's no chance you'll say "No" when they hand you the pen to sign your approval.

Chapter 5

A Business Profit-Planning Primer

Let's start right off with finding out what business planning is.

> *"Planning" is deciding NOW—*
> *Which operating conditions to change TODAY—*
> *So that performance results TOMORROW—*
> *Will be favorably different from YESTERDAY.*

All in all, that's not a bad definition. I hope that the principal message you get is that, first and foremost, planning is an exercise in anticipation.

Far too often, "planning" is viewed as an event, an episode, or an act. "It's time to *do* planning." "He *does* our planning." "Aw c'mon, enough planning already. Let's get back to *work*." You've all heard those statements, haven't you? What's that? Some of you have actually uttered them? Shame! Shame! First of all, I have never read a professionally prepared Job Description for any operating management position that failed to include, "prepare appropriate supporting PLANS" or words to that effect. Once you make the transition from "doer" or "delegee" to "manager" or "delegator," planning is a necessary ingredient of the substantive content of the new job.

Planning is certainly *not* an event, nor is it an episode. At the very least, it is a "process." At best, it is a "mind-set."

> *The prime attribute of successful (that is, effective) planning is the ability to identify quickly an end result acceptable to the affected parties.*

The requisite mental attitude of any successful planner, or successful manager, for that matter, is to quickly, dispassionately and quantitatively define the desired end result—the operational bull's-eye. There are only three required words which capture this truly crucial, pivotal characteristic:

> *Last is first!*

How many of you play chess? C'mon. Raise your hands. That many, eh? Well, let me tell you that 98.325 percent of you learned to play chess in the most incorrect sequence imaginable. Further, unless you change your ways, you are doomed to be, at best, only a mediocre "wood pusher." First, you learned how each piece moved, right? Then you concentrated on the openings? You might have even bought some books on chess openings. Right? Then you hurried to start to play. Nothing like "cross the board play and all that." NONSENSE! There is only one way to learn to play chess.

The objective of the game is to checkmate or capture your opponent's King. Checkmate means that (a) your opponent's King will be captured in the very next move, and (b) there is no way (of the three possible ways) your opponent can prevent you from making that next move, can prevent the capture of his King. There are less than 150 different ways to checkmate your opponent's King— to WIN the game. So the very best (again, that is, the most effective) way to begin to learn to play chess is to— what else?—learn the ways to kill off your opponent's King.

The lesson is both simple and inescapable. The most effective way to learn to win is to master, first, the END-INGS! *Last is first!* Once you've mastered them, learn the so-called middle-game, which leads you to the already familiar endings. *Finally,* learn the "openings" which, in turn, get you to the already mastered end-game!

> *Don't even think about beginning* anything *until you really know where you want it to end up. You* must *start your thinking and planning* always *and* only *by quantifying the circumstances or objective or result that you ultimately want to eventuate.*

Until you can measurably define your ultimate objective or goal, you don't understand it well enough to warrant taking any action toward it. It's as simple as that. It's also as tough as that. It's really a most challenging task. You have to place yourself out into the future, then foresee *and* measure as many parameters as you can. Remember: You will not have taken a single action yet toward that goal. But you can rest assured that the better, the more thorough, more detailed, more quantitatively specific job that you initially do, the far more likely it is that your plan will be effective and your objective(s) will be achieved.

PLANNING = MANAGING = PLANNING = MANAGING = . . .

As we all know—after the insightful, crystal-clear exposition in Chapter 3—management means getting work done through the efforts of others. Certainly one of the key, cardinal prerequisites to successful management is the obligation by subordinates that they really *are* expected to *do* (whatever) *by* (whenever). And it must be more than only a realization; it must be more than a perception. It must be a burr under their saddle. It must be the small voice that keeps telling them, "You had better get moving." It must be that gnawing concern that leads them to skip lunch just this once; to get to the office at 6:30 A.M. to make sure they've got a head start; to work on Saturday once in a while when the need arises—without being asked (or told to). It must become a disciplinary imperative. It must be a driving force. It must become an integral ingredient of behavior pattern.

Some people have named that approach Management by Expectation. Others refer to the requisite of vulnerability of the subordinates. I prefer to talk about *Management by Measurement and Accountability*. Both criteria are crucial. Measurement is an absolute prerequisite necessity; without it there can be absolutely no accountability at all. As I've said elsewhere, "While plans by their very nature are transitory and short-lived, they are nonetheless commitments to measured performance."* The key word, from an operating management viewpoint, is "commitment," because with-

---

* *No-Nonsense Planning*, The Free Press, 1984, p. 5.

out commitment there cannot even begin to be the semblance of accountability. And it is upon accountability that effective performance is premised.

If the delegee or subordinate feels no obligation to perform, the results, at best, will be mediocre. It is the sting of the obligation to perform, the prospect of potential embarrassment in the presence of one's peers and colleagues that triggers that extra shot of adrenaline which so stirs the blood. The obligation to perform stems, too, from the personal conviction that one's performance can indeed be excellent; and, further, your conviction that your superior so believes in you that he expects you to achieve high levels of performance. Both sticks and carrots. Carrots move the "self-starters"; sticks are for the rest of us.

There is no question but that the level of managerial performance is directly related to the degree of enthusiasm, the "can-do" content, the intensity of the élan that the manager brings to the task, the challenge, the opportunity. This valuable insight provides the basis for the most cogent, critical, and important advice that I can give to the "new" operations manager or the old hand facing a "new" challenge:

> *Spend* no *time or effort making "little" plans.*
> *They have no magic to stir men's blood—or to*
> *make owners as wealthy as they could be!*

Keynes recognized this principle long ago. One of his keystone concepts was that "big projects" arouse an absolutely essential ingredient in the capitalist process. Rationality? No, not at all. He called that ingredient "animal spirits," connoting a visceral compulsion.

Thus, because successful management is contingent upon the presence of a vital, throbbing, driving sense of accountability, and, . . . because the existence of accountability is dependent upon the formalization of commitments to measured performance, and, . . . because the planning process, if professionally performed, culminates in formalized commitments to measured performance; it follows as night the day:

Planning = Managing = Planning = Managing = . . .

THE ART OF MANAGEMENT

In my view, this section could very well be the most important one in this (or any other) business management book. Certainly it is one of the cardinal concepts that I deeply hope you will take from this book and incorporate in your daily business management life. Please study (don't just peruse) this section carefully. It will be worth your while, you'll see.

Our colleagues quickly agree that management is both "an art and a science." It's always a blend, you see. The proportions, unfortunately, are never fixed or even specified. The nature or characteristics of the "art" and/or the "science" are never carefully defined or even listed. What most people mean by that loose label is that managers sometimes act more emotionally than logically or rationally (the "art") and, at other times, act more rationally than emotionally (voila! "science"). There is almost a universal "linkage" between "art" as named as a component of management and "people-handling," "interpersonal dynamics," "chemistry," and "humanism."

A great deal of ado is expended on the "art" side of management. And why not? Proponents, supporters, practitioners, and other assorted afficianados will quickly, even if imprecisely, tell you that, after all!, *people* is what it's all about. And, therefore, it simply must be impossible to say too much about the "art" of management. Books, articles, seminars, tapes, "training" sessions, and meetings abound. It is a rare mail delivery indeed that fails to include at least one slick, multicolored combination ad and enrollment form. Personnel managers have been magically metamorphosed into Human Resource Managers. (Strictly between you and me, I'm convinced that the former title connotes a far less nonhuman and commodity-type approach to people than does the latter.) Never mind that the language and methodology is so loose that serious doubt exists that anyone really knows anymore what exactly it is they are talking about. Never mind that the "pursuit of artiness" is so popular, attracts so many followers. It is, after all, a whopping great deal of innocent fun. If everything is expressed in catchy adjectives and adverbs, there is no way at all that you can be held accountable for anything! And since all of this stuff consists of unverifiable opinions anyway, then one's opinion must be just as good, just as valid as anyone else's, right? So if you need a break from the grind, attend an "artsy" seminar. You'll enjoy! It's all heady stuff, guaranteed. Ofttimes you will plumb the profundity depths of civil rights, employees' rights, women's rights, minorities' rights, apprentices' rights, drug addicts' rights, criminals' rights, and a whole range of other ''rights'' with but one glaring exception: the *rights of the owners!*

Since the attendees are not owners (with but rare exception), why waste any time considering their rights? Rather, you can focus exclusively on new and better ways to spend their money. And you'll feel great because it's all done under the noble banner of improving people-relations, of glossing the corporate governance image, of advancing the frontiers of ''humanism.'' I ask those of you who so expend time and effort that, with rare exception, every single dollar you spend, directly or indirectly, belongs to the owners of the firm. When was the last time the owners, directly, told you it was okay to so spend a bunch of their bucks? Okay, enough about ''art.'' Why is the ''science'' of management important to talk about in this book?

THE SCIENCE OF MANAGEMENT

In one sentence: Effective, rigorous dedicated PLANNING is a disciplined, quantitative iteration of cause and effect (the essential ''stuff'' of all science), but it is performed in reverse!

> *Planning* is *management science and the science of management* is *planning!*

If there is any science at all involved in business management, it is embodied in the planning process. *All* of Operations Research (so-called) Management Science or Strategic Modeling is nothing more or less than Planning. It is always the same algorithm or procedure.

Step (1) Quantitatively (when, how much, where, etc.) define the operational circumstances that you plan to eventuate.

Step (2) thru N. Step-by-step, one-by-one, quantitatively define or describe the causal circumstances that must exist just prior to the desired "result" or set of operational circumstances.

Let's look at it graphically:

```
                                          (1) Effect
                          (2) Cause ──────→ (1) Effect
          (3) Effect ──────→ (2) Cause ──────→ (1) Effect
(4) Cause ──────→ (3) Effect ──────→ (2) Cause ──────→ (1) Effect
```

1. *Start at the end!* This describes/defines the *ultimate* planned Effect.

2. These are the operational, real-world actions and *must* be executed so there will be a high probability that (1) Effect *will* occur *as planned*.

3. Same as (1) above.

4. Same as (2) above.

and so on and so on . . . backing up, step-by-step, from the future to the present.

Another way to look at the science of management:

```
                                           (1) Results
                          (2) Actions ──────→ (1) Results
          (3) Results ──────→ (2) Actions ──────→ (1) Results
(4) Actions──────→ (3) Results ──────→ (2) Actions ──────→ (1) Results
```

Finally, if you substitute "Results" for "Effect" and "Actions" for "Cause," you've got the essence of the science of management. "Actions → Results" equals, in every way, the now familiar "Cause → Effect" couplet.

Planning, then, is the formulation of a series of quantitative statements that begin with "Results" and then define the "Actions" that must be taken to generate the desired objective goal or planned "Results." Now, Webster defines scientific method as: "principles and procedures for the systematic pursuit of knowledge involving the recognition and formulation of a problem, the collection of data through observation and equipment, and the formulation and testing of hypotheses."

Let's explore how the scientific method is (must be) incorporated in effective business planning. We begin by modifying the "Actions → Results" planning logic chain.

$$
\begin{aligned}
&\text{(1) Results} \\
&\text{(2) Actions} \rightleftharpoons \text{(1) Results} \\
&\text{(3) Results} \rightleftharpoons \text{(2) Actions} \rightleftharpoons \text{(1) Results} \\
&\text{(4) Actions} \rightleftharpoons \text{(3) Results} \rightleftharpoons \text{(2) Actions} \rightleftharpoons \text{(1) Results}
\end{aligned}
$$

Note that the change is the addition of a "feedback" arrow. Thus, while the planning process defines the one-way (downstream) direction of intended action and consequential results, the management function of monitoring and control is signified by the "upstream" arrow. Don't misinterpret the term "downstream," to be synonymous with the planning process. That is, do *not* infer that the planning process is a one-way, top-down, the boss will give you the numbers exercise. The professionally performed planning process is always participatory—a team effort. More on this a little later.

What is meant here is that the objective of the planning

process is to quantitatively define all of the intermediary results (and their respective prerequisite actions) such that there is a probability far in excess of 50 percent that the desired final Results will eventuate if the successive Action/Result logic modules are professionally executed.

The management monitoring and control upstream arrow denotes the flow of feedback comparative data. The results actually obtained are compared to (a) the planned results *and* (b) the planned actions. These evaluations tell professionals, first, how close they came to what they planned the results to be, and, second, the degree of effectiveness of the planned action.

By now you must be impressed with the unparalleled importance I place on EXECUTION. But just in case it may have escaped your notice, execution is almost (not quite, but very close) as important as PLANNING itself. Planning *must* have the priority edge. If not, undisciplined execution too closely resembles an unguided missile. The degree to which the entire planning process is rigorously and aggressively executed separates the few management ''pro's'' from the hordes of the ''also-rans.''

PROFESSIONALISM IN MANAGEMENT

Webster tells us that a profession is ''a calling requiring specialized knowledge and often long intensive academic preparation. . . .'' A professional, he goes on, is one ''characterized by or conforming to the technical standards of a profession.''

The conception, formulation, documentation, and implementation of an effective, motivating, self-monitoring plan does *indeed* require "specialized knowledge" and "conformance to technical . . . standards." But perhaps even more important, the planner—to be truly outstanding, a real "pro"—must bring enthusiasm, élan, and a will to win to the task. Mere "to the letter" lip service will not suffice here any more than it would in any other profession. *The person who must rely on a cookbook will never a chef be!* True excellence stems from the "soul," the spirit, the genuine, unblemished, undiluted, sincere interest and concern spawned by a compelling urge to master and excel! You know, as you think about it, "excellence" is NEVER *results;* it is always a never-ending quest that drives the achievement of results.

Bottom line of all this? ONLY "planning" provides legitimacy to the claim that management is *both* a science *and* a profession.

PLANNING MAXIMIZES EXECUTIVE PRODUCTIVITY

We all know that management meetings are usually a pain in the dorsal terminus. According to a recent authoritative survey of executives from a hundred firms, an estimated 16.5 hours per week is spent in meetings and that 29 percent (roughly a third) of that time is a total waste and often counterproductive. That amounts to more than six weeks per year that are both wasteful and damaging for the firm. First, money is expended to prepare for and conduct the meetings, and, second, nothing of value results from those expenditures.

We all also know that only TIME is the true enemy! Not competition, not government rules and regulations. So it follows that the least amount of time that is wasted, the better. Thus, poorly managed meetings not only fail to get results and waste dollars, more unforgiveably, they waste irretrievable TIME.

Why are meetings so unproductive? Why is so much time and money wasted? Did God decide that this is the way it must be? No, of course not. There is only one place to look, and one person to hold accountable for the success, or lack thereof, of management meetings. That one place is the Chair and that one person is its occupant— the person who convened the meeting in the first place. But merely finger-pointing at culpability provides absolutely no curative remedy. I truly like the old saw that instructs us, "Whenever you point your finger at someone, you point three of them right back at yourself." Let's be more causally specific, shall we?

Far too many meetings are only "get-togethers." They tend to be too informal, too ethereal, too long, and too bad. Again, however, I'm being more descriptive than definitional, aren't I? Why are meetings generally so characterized? First, meetings tend to be unorganized and undisciplined. Too often, invitees are unaware of (a) what the subject or purpose of the meeting is and (b) what their respective role is expected to be. When a meeting is convened, the productivity loss begins because of the lack, absence, void of organization and discipline. Given these shortages, managerial anarchy is the inescapable result.

Professional business managers (at least all those so titled) and Mother Nature have one very important thing in common: They both abhor a vacuum. When one is sensed, they both launch forces to fill the void. In a business meeting, if the attendees (at least those who aspire to higher-level management positions) perceive an organizational gap, they will leap to fill it with arguments which champion their own current "hot" projects. If this first fault is further compounded by a dearth of discipline, the field is open to the glib, the articulate, and the politicians (God and shareholders forgive us!).

There are, not surprisingly, only a few requirements to avoid meeting unproductivity, to improve management effectiveness and productivity by some 10–15 percent! First, use a *fixed agenda*. NO, not the same agenda for every meeting, just the same agenda for *each type* of meeting. This practice firmly establishes the permissable parameters beyond which attendee "hot dogs" dare not go.

Second, use *fixed formats* of reporting and/or desired participation. Again, the formats vary to reflect the purpose of the meeting, but they should always be the same for each type of meeting.

Third, open each meeting with a brief description/reminder of the explicit purpose(s) of the meeting. Remind the attendees why they are there and what is expected of them while they are there. Elementary? Presumable? Certainly! Yet, the frequency with which these basics are overlooked is frightening and—worse yet—unprofitable! The shareholders are getting gypped! And as a professional manager, that infuriates me.

So much for the theory of improving management productivity. Practical, complete, how-to implementational details will be found in Chapters 4 and 9.

THE SCIENCE OF MANAGEMENT FACILITATES THE ART OF MANAGEMENT

The "art" of management revolves about the nebulous concept of "people skills," as we earlier learned it was commonly termed. The "art" of "people skills" is gaining in importance, at least so say the well-published pundits. I have yet to hear a confirming chorus from owners, however. Why do problems of people-skills arise at all? That's simple. People-skills refers to the management and control of relationships between individual people. The achievement and maintenance of people-skill is difficult, indeed, but why is it *so* difficult?

Well, the answer can be simply stated: The individuals involved in the relationships change frequently and often without control by either of the parties. In turn, the causes of the changes in the rosters of individuals are many, varied, and familiar. Among the more important are: starting a new job, a promotion, a demotion, merger, acquisition, plant (office) closing or opening, termination, lay-off, and reassignment. Of course, in many cases, these causes can occur in customers' and/or vendors' firms and result in interpersonal changes that your employees will face.

Now, how, exactly, does the science of planning and incremental gain facilitate the practice of the art of people-skills? Since the primal source of interpersonal problems is the conflict or incompatibility of personalities, any force or technique which reduces focus on personality will mitigate the severity of the people-skill problems. The focus, priority, and undivided attention of management personnel is centered on the business issues—the problems and opportunities—and the action necessary to either solve or exploit them.

Rewards and punishment (that is, the treatment of business personnel) should be meted out only according to the performance results achieved by each individual with *no* reliance on "personality." Management would be more effective if each employee was treated in a no-nonsense, businesslike manner, irrespective of race, sex, religion, or national origin; if each person was tendered respect, dignity, and stature according to objectively measured performance; and if each individual was treated with humanity, with neither malice nor pity.

ANATOMIZE: THEN SYNTHESIZE

Most frequently, as I speak and conduct seminars across the country, I am asked, "Where does one begin the professional, effective business planning process?" There already has been acceptance of the notion that business profit planning is, if it is indeed anything else, a prolonged exercise in (if the truth be known, only elementary) logic. As a matter of fact, when approached properly, planning is a series of tiresome, unglamorous, plodding steps. It's a lot more fun to, say, take an important customer out to dinner (or maybe even not *so* important a customer as one with whom we get along very well), or even to tour the friendly confines of the plant of a favored vendor. When you come right down to it, and if the truth be known (really!), planning is downright tedious. And that's why (honest!) so many otherwise competent operating managers go to such great lengths to avoid (Yuck!) "planning."

But let's say we're dealing with an operating manager who sincerely (one of the rare ones) wants to at least know how and where to begin the business planning process. Just like *you*, right? I hope so! *You begin by quantitatively describing/defining the array of performance results that you want to eventuate,* and *when you want them to eventuate*.

Suppose you're dealing with, say, Net Sales. You want to post sales of $1 million by year's end. Now, that statement, by itself, is merely an objective, a goal. Yet you will encounter too many managers who try to palm it off as a Plan. "That's my plan, boss, to get $1 million in sales this year." Ever hear that? Sure. Ever say that? Hmmm!

To make a meaningful, useful Plan, you have simply got to start breaking the ultimate goal down into digestible manageable "chunks," or units. You will see how these units tie together with objectives in Chapter 9. As you begin your analysis *please* remember how Webster defines an analysis. It is *not* a REPORT, for God's sake! It is the "separation of a whole into its component parts"! Remember that Sales are *always* the *result* of operational activity, of production activity. Too often, there is confusion between the respective functions of the Sales Department and the Production Department. The function of the Sales Department is *not* to obtain sales! The function of the Sales Department is to obtain ORDERS—ideally, profitable and readily collectible orders. The function of the Production Department is to effect SALES—ideally in conformance to the specifications of the order, within cost parameters, on time, and embodying at least adequate levels of quality.

Our analysis or anatomization begins by meting out the $1 million of annual sales into monthly amounts. By the way, let's clear up the crucial difference between "analysis" and "anatomization." Again, Webster tells us that "anatomization" is: "dissecting the parts . . . to ascertain their [relative] position, relation, structure and function."

So we go farther and deeper with anatomization than with mere analysis. The experienced amateur planner, in the at-hand case, would surely allocate sales by month. But he would usually stop there. And by stopping there, he thereby condemns the result of the planning activity to the fate we have all seen far too frequently, namely, a nicely bound volume on the bookshelf of the boardroom. There is an almost audible, collective, "Whew, that was a near miss!" from the organization as that paltry sales volume is installed as *the* objective.

On the other hand, the "pro" *starts* with a monthly allocation of annual sales, *then the real planning work only just begins*. A series of questions will help you to grasp the methodology.

Q 1. What are the relative contributions to the $1 million of increased sales from each product line?

Q 2. What are the relative contributions to the increase of $1 million by each salesperson and/or channel of distribution?

Q 3. How much of the $1 million is generated by established customers, by new customers? Just how effective is the 80–20 rule (or Pareto's Law)?

These three questions are usually enough to at least illustrate the process for you. In your particular firm you will undoubtedly generate many more questions. They should be carefully drafted and numerous enough to adequately define/describe the quantitative desired results. This is very important, because:

> *It is from answers to these questions that incentive compensation performance objectives will be derived and defined!*

The answers to these questions are derived by participatory involvement of the functional managers and other appropriate key personnel. Active participation is both necessary and assured. It is assured because once the initial answers have been obtained, the interrogative dialogue proceeds to (a) test reasonability, and (b) establish "ownership" of the obligation to perform. NOTE: What is meant by (b) is the avoidance of legitimacy of the claim by subordinates that "That's NOT *my* number; the Boss just gave it to me—period."

Again, let's use the answer to Question 1 above to illustrate the reasonability or sanity testing phases. Let's say that the initial answer to Question 1 is "50 percent line A, 25 percent each product lines B and C." We then proceed to test reasonability.

R 1. Does the historical pattern of sales support or mirror this pattern?

If *not,* R 2. What is the demonstrable evidence that this new pattern will eventuate? . . . and so on.

If *so,* R 8. When must the orders be booked such that the planned sales have more than a 50–50 chance, in the time allowed, of being produced and invoiced?

R 9. What are the respective cycle-times from "booked order-to-shipment" for each product line?

R 10. Is there a greater than 50–50 likelihood of booking the appropriate orders within the time constraints?

Thus, the subordinate (the Sales Department Manager in this case) is led, step-by-step, to the deeper, more complete and quantitative understanding of the performance result objectives that he faces. These become "his" numbers. He *has,* in fact, participated!

A complementary approach often proves of great value. It is called the OPS approach, or Objective/Problem/Solution. I have found this to be a particularly useful technique with operating managers who are putting a professional plan together for the first time. It works this way. First, the Objective is quantitatively described in terms of amount, date, etc. Then the planner defines the Problem(s) that stands in the way of achieving the Objective. In other words, if there were *no* definable obstacles to achievement, the Objective is too timid, too low, too insufficient, too suboptimal. In fact, with nothing barring the way, we should *already* be there, shouldn't we? Finally, the planner then defines the Solution (the action or series of actions) that must be executed such that its corresponding Problem will be "solved" so that, in turn, the Objective will be reached.

Let's move on to "Synthesis," shall we? Webster again is our principal guide: "The composition or confirmation of often diverse parts, elements or conceptions into a coherent whole." This concept is particularly useful for operating management because the task facing the chief operating officer is *always* how to best combine the efforts of the various organizational functions (sales, production, finance, engineering, and so on) which are usually, at least to some degree, in conflict, such that the enduring value of the shareholders' investment is enhanced.

This is the stage that is most challenging to the chief operating officer. The problem can be easily stated, "Arrive at only those objectives which, if the operating managers aggressively pursue the letter, will (a) avoid counterproductive results, and, simultaneously, (b) additively meet/exceed the desired performance results for the firm." First, an example of the counterproductive type of objectives. A lesson in learning what *not* to do! An operations vice president I once knew offered a bonus to the production planners if they could substantially cut inventory. So far so good. However, he failed to explore the results of his directive/incentive when taken to the extremes. He placed no conditions or qualifications on the payment of the bonus; simply, he told them to cut inventory and if they did they would be paid a bonus. Simple as that. If you or I were a production planner, we'd go precisely where the most bonus dollars could be made, right? So, they, just as you or I, went immediately to the "A" items—you know, those are the ones that are most frequently used, have the greatest usage. Well, the production planners cancelled *all* the incoming orders of the "A" items. Predictably, sure enough, as the on-shelf "A" items were used up in product assembly and those products were shipped, inventory levels did, indeed, go down. And the production planners did, indeed, receive their bonuses. But, *BUT,* the chief operating officer then had to explain to the Board why bonuses were paid to the production planners when the plant was closing down and customers were finding other sources because of multiple key parts outages!

In other words, it IS difficult to arrive at objectives that, at the same time, strongly encourage individual managers to aggressively pursue their own personal, selfish ends, and yet are well enough thought out so that even when taken only literally and executed only to the letter they *nevertheless* successfully *combine* to yield increasingly favorable results for the owners. NOTE: I said it is difficult. Not impossible, only difficult. It is *not* a severely complex, mysterious, or esoteric task.

Why, then, do owner-managers and employee-managers so strenuously shy away from even initiating an MBO (Management by Objectives) program? First of all, the owners may not really desire to maximize their financial return on investment. And because they are the owners, after all, they're entitled to prefer greater psychic return on their investment (see Chapter 2). Second, it is not a bad thing to be reluctant to initiate those activities in which we are inexpert. On the other hand, if one's goal is to maximize profit, financial return on investment, and the enduring value of the shareholders' investment, then there is *no* valid excuse for failure to engage expert assistance to quickly and effectively initiate and install an MBO—an Incentive Compensation Program consistent with the concepts of managing by increment.

In conclusion, there is *always* a way to predetermine measurable performance results. You, personally, may not be aware of all of them, but your ignorance or inexperience is not a valid argument to support inaction and/or procrastination. If—and it is a crucially important "if,"—your aim *is* to maximize financial return on investment, profit, and the enduring value of the shareholders' investment, then you must focus on incremental gains!

"LESS" REALLY IS ALWAYS "MORE"!

Become intimately familiar with the notion of a "unit of change." As we've seen, the unit of change is also called an increment. But further and more importantly, there is a supremely valuable concept that all too often is simply totally overlooked. Namely:

> *The smaller the unit of change, the smaller the increment, the better!*

It is far easier to effect a 2 percent sales price increase than a 10 percent one. It is far easier to reduce material cost by 2 percent than, say, 5 percent. It is far easier to eliminate five jobs than fifty. And so on. You get the idea?

It is a far more "reasonable" demand of operating managers to implement a 2 percent sales price increase than a 10 percent one. It is a far more "reasonable" demand of operating management to implement a 2 percent reduction in material cost than a 5 percent one. It is a far more "reasonable" demand of operating management to eliminate five jobs than fifty. And so on.

It is far easier to keep track of 2 percent changes than 10 percent or even five percent changes, is it not? It is less upsetting to an organization if only five jobs are eliminated rather than fifty. Again, and so on.

You've got the idea, I'm sure. The smaller the "bite," the easier it is to swallow and digest. From that eye-opening, powerful yet deceptively simple truth come five important, useful, and compelling inferences.

Inference 1

The smaller the increment of change, the shorter becomes the control cycle; and the more effective, thereby, becomes management control.

As defined on page 34 of my book *No-Nonsense Management,* "A control cycle is the time that it takes to conceive, document, approve, implement and assess the results—of a decision." And I went on to say, "The longer the control cycle, the greater the likelihood that an intervening development will (impair) control focus."

Thus, as more objectives are defined as "Increase sales price of Product Lines A, C, and G by 2 percent by the end of the first quarter," rather than "Increase prices by 15 percent," personal control is enhanced for each accountable manager.

Inference 2

The smaller the increment of change, the easier it is to measure as both an objective and on an interim progress basis.

The measurement becomes easier, first, because there is less exposure to distortion from the intrusion of uncontrollable exogenous variables, such as those forces external to the firm and generally untouchable by the firm's operating management. Second, the smaller the change to be measured, the less likely it is that implementation of the change will entail crossing of organizational or functional lines. Thus, since the change tends to be "compartmentalized," it can more easily be measured and tracked.

Inference 3

The smaller the increment of change, the more easily and the quicker it can be understood.

To anyone who has ever conducted a class, chaired a seminar, or even delivered a speech, it will be painfully remembered that "The mind can absorb only what the (dorsal terminus) can endure." Also, the more complicated the logic chain, the less likely it is that the listener can stay with the presenter from beginning to end. It is axiomatic that the smaller the demand placed on a span of attention, the more likely it is that the message will be successfully transmitted.

It is always easier to understand, to absorb information when it is served up in bite-sized chunks rather than in one long, three-foot hero sandwich. That's why all books are comprised of chapters, sections, paragraphs, and, even, sentences. No need to belabor this point, right?

CUMULATIVE Inference 1

Based upon the earlier Inferences, the smaller the increment of change, the more easily enthused one can become about achieving it.

This is but another way of saying that a manager *can* be motivated to achieve higher, predetermined performance levels as (a) he has greater control over his task(s), (b) he can easily and routinely measure *both* his objective *and* his interim progress, (c) he understands *what* is expected of him, and (d) *when* it is expected.

While there may be many and varied forces at work at any given time affecting the outcome of human endeavor, none is more potent or lasting than the fervor, the drive, the élan that even one, single inspired individual can bring. In a word, it is called "motivation." The old plaintive chorus, "Give me ten stout-hearted men and I'll soon give you 10,000 more," is *NOT* without operating management wisdom or application.

How often it is the case that even a Superbowl victory is secured by the team who "wants it most." Enthusiasm and motivation are *so* closely allied that they are, in effect, interchangeable for our purposes. Thus, the smaller the increment, the greater the motivational power there is to achieve it!

CUMULATIVE Inference 2

The smaller the increment of change, the more likely it is that the objective will be achieved!

Finally, the payoff inference! Given all of the earlier step-by-step inferential evidence, there is no conclusionary inference that could be more compelling or more obvious. As stated earlier, "An inch is a cinch, a yard is hard!"

While that proposition easily appealed to your common sense, this chain of inferential logic explains, in somewhat more verifiable terms, how we got there.

PLAN ONLY THAT WHICH THE OWNERS WANT TO ACHIEVE

I harken back to Chapter 2. If you are an owner and know what it is you want, then go out of your way to motivate your operating management to prepare and implement plans to achieve it. If you are an owner and are not really sure how much financial return on investment you want, then stand aside and let operating management fulfill their professional obligation—to maximize the enduring value of your investment. It is always easier, isn't it, to limit or reduce the amount of operating profit than it is to increase it. So if you're not sure what you want done, it's always better to make more profit than less while you're making up your mind, right?

On the other hand, as an operating manager, your primary function is to effectively manage change. Your mission, absent direction otherwise from the owners, is to maximize financial return on their investment, to enhance the enduring value of the shareholders' investment. A plan, if it is anything, represents—usually CAUSES—change. Your primary obligation is to see to it that whatever changes occur are consistent with and supportive of the wants of the owners.

It requires time and expense to prepare a complete business or profit plan. And remember, you are spending the *owners'* time and money. Therefore, *any* expenditure of owners' time and money which is inconsistent or in conflict with the owners' wants, desires, and interests could easily be viewed as malfeasance in office. Not only is a disservice done to the owners, it usually will not be long before they (just as you and I would, in their shoes) say, "Enough is enough. Goodbye and good luck."

In sum, this point seems *so* painfully obvious. Why take your time to even raise it and talk a little about it? Because it is also *so* frequently and pervasively overlooked, ignored, and/or unappreciated. Owners are subject to extensive disservice; millions of their dollars are "wasted" in the legal sense. Far too many employee-managers, left too much to themselves, will generally form an elitist bureaucracy, intent on perpetuation and enlargement. They will award themselves "cushy" perks; they will live the life of the corporate "prince." You, just as much as I, have seen this phenomenon and have met such employee-managers. Maybe you even worked side-by-side with them. Maybe you are one of them. So remember, the higher the position that you currently hold in the firm, the more demanding, rigorous, and profound is your duty and obligation to do those (legal) things that the *owners* want done! Oh, sure, it is expected that you will suggest, recommend, and propose. But go no farther with significant expenditures of time or money without the endorsement, support, approval of the people who sign your payroll check—the OWNERS!

Remembering that it is impossible to argue with success, I leave you with the pithy, cogent admonition of movie mogul Samuel Goldwyn (no less): "Never make forecasts, especially about the future."

SECTION II

PRACTICING MANAGEMENT BY INCREMENTAL GAINS

In the next four chapters you will be supplied with all the nitty-gritty, practical procedural detail to successfully manage by incremental gains.

All I can do is make this material available to you. We both know that. I have tried to present it clearly and concisely. If you have questions or problems with this section, please write to me at your convenience. What, exactly, does Section II have in store for you? Let's take an overview.

In Chapter 6, I anatomize the functional operating management challenges that face us to meet/exceed the owners' demands for operating pre-tax profit. By the way, let's agree, shall we, that "*Objectives* of Performance" means the very same thing as "*Results* of Performance," and has NOTHING to do with (merely) effort, exertion, attempt, or tenure. What we're talking about in Chapter 6 (and 7, 8, and 9, for that matter) is operational results gleaned from the "ongoing" business. We are *not* concerned with

116

LIFO-FIFO reserve transfers, "one-time" impacts, and the like. In other words, forget the "nicky-nocky" of "numbers massage." What I'm concerned with and what you, as operating management *should* be concerned with, is the pre-tax profit that the organization (that is, the "firm") is generating and will, most likely, generate in the future from the basic, ongoing business.

In Chapter 7, I will do for planning, monitoring, and control of cash flow what I did for operating pre-tax in Chapter 6. You will generally find it to be the case that the smaller the firm, the more interested and concerned the owners are about operating cash flow vis-à-vis operating pre-tax.

In Chapter 8, you will find yet another "first" in operating management and control! It is generally accepted—at expensive seminars, lunches, and dinners—that some 30–40¢ of each and every Sales Dollar is spent on employees either directly or indirectly! This, then, is clearly the largest slice of the firm's negative cash flow. And yet, honestly now, aren't you simply amazed at the extensive inattention that is given to this crucial cash flow? Well, I sure as hell am!

There is always at least one course in every graduate school of business that deals with employee compensation. But you will never find a course in any business school as useful and effective ("increasing the enduring value of the shareholders' investment") as Chapter 8!

As far as I know, this is the *first* (and *only*) attempt by operating management to put, all in one place, the cost of people! Sure, people are our most important asset. How can you *not* believe it? But somehow, when it comes to considering and assessing the expense of people, we forget that the owners simply must be served. Chapter 8 provides the implementational procedure to analyze, control, and plan all of employee compensation expenses.

And finally, we come to Chapter 9. My unquestioned favorite chapter! And it will be yours, too. In this capstone chapter, I provide you with BOTH the "stick" and the "carrot." As far as I'm concerned, the "stick" is *not* a punishment system; it's a program of measured discipline. A Control and Reporting System, if it is anything, must be a reliable, dependable procedure whereby a person who is serious about achieving results can self-audit his performance progress and that of his peers as well! You will be presented with a complete "package": Criteria for Effectiveness; Agendas for Meetings; forms; procedures; *and* instructions.

The "carrot," well, that's something else again. It is, it *must* be (to be effective), a genuine reward system. It is the financial extension of the psychological principle of behavioral reinforcement. The better the results, the greater the reward should be. You, again, will be presented with a complete implementational "package." The criteria with which to measure program effectiveness, evaluation, concepts, definitions, explanatory prose, payment formulae, forms, and so on. You will see how the Incentive Compensation Program is integrated and embodies within the Control and Reporting Systems.

The chart Practicing Management by Incremental Gains (Figure 2) presents, on only one page for your reading convenience, a most useful *overview and summary of all of Section II*. Make a copy of that page and use it as a

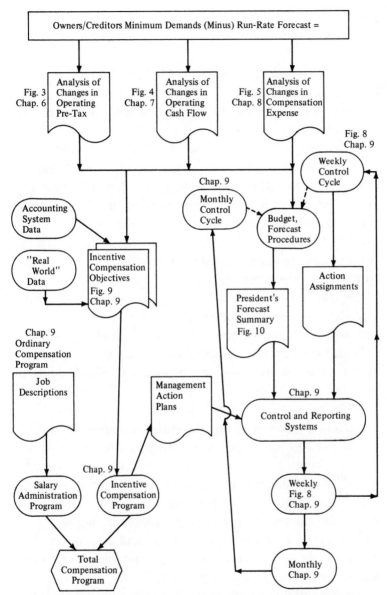

Figure 2. Practicing Management by Incremental Gains

bookmark as you proceed through the chapters. Keep it handy and study it when you have free moments—in airline waiting rooms, etc. Get to the point where you can sketch it from memory.

It all starts with a measurement of the performance "difference" between what the owners/creditors want and the results that will most likely occur if we don't make any major changes in the operating environment. That "difference" is then incrementally defined in the three key documents. The ONLY three areas of serious management concern are: operating pre-tax, operating cash flow, and employee compensation.

The second major area of concern to the professional manager answers the question, "How can I communicate and monitor progress; how can I Control and Report?"

Both the Weekly and Monthly Cycles are installed not only to support, but also to enhance the effectiveness of the Control and Reporting System.

Of important note is the interface of the Control and Reporting System with the Incentive Compensation Program! Far too often, you will find that even if these two systems/programs exist in a firm at all, they are *not* integrated so that the sum effect of the two is greater than the parts! Merely quantifying the "difference" in performance is, by far, nowhere near enough! Incorporating the ways and means to *keep* operating management current on diagnoses *and* prognoses is indisputable. And when those diagnoses and prognoses are, hopefully, favorable, or regrettably otherwise, the impact on incentive compensation (and perhaps even ordinary compensation) must be quantitatively assessed.

As you can see, the prime motivational force for achievement of the tasks required to bridge the performance gap or "difference" is tied to the Financial Factors of Motivation. And this is a vital tie-in, indeed! More than 95 percent of the time, more than 95 percent of management personnel will be more than 95 percent motivated to perform at higher performance levels that are needed to achieve more than 95 percent of the total desired result!

Not too bad, eh? I know hundreds of owners/creditors who would "sign up" to get that result at the drop of a hat!

How can the untrained eye discern that you have been successful in your efforts to motivate your organization, your personnel? It's too early, say, to actually measure the differences in the firm's performance results, but you'd still like to be able to tell whether the management corps has, in fact, been turned on. I'm sure that there are some tried and true psychological tests that can be administered to obtain useful insights and inferences. I have found out over the years that it's really not necessary to get all that formal. And, besides, it would take time and it would cost money.

No, *I've found it useful to look for just one trait, just one behavioral display: enthusiasm.* Or, to use a term that I really much more prefer, *hustle!* I like to use *hustle!* because it's so easy to get the meaning across. After all, can't you just see Mr. Hustle, himself, Pete Rose, doing one of his patented head-first slides into third base?

Let's see if we can give a more complete description of what *hustle!* really is.

- *Hustle!* is believing in yourself and the business you're in.
- *Hustle!* is doing something that everyone is absolutely certain cannot be done.
- *Hustle!* is the sheer joy of *winning!*
- *Hustle!* is being the absolutely sorest loser in town.
- *Hustle!* is getting the order because you got there first— or because you stayed with it after everyone else gave up.
- *Hustle!* is getting prospects to say "yes" after they've said "no" twenty times.
- *Hustle!* is hating to go out for lunch or take a vacation because you might miss some of the action.

Think you can spot a "hustling" management team when you see one? Of course you can—*now!* And when you do see one, sense one, feel one, you can rest assured that the firms's financial performance results will improve both greatly and soon!

Finally, I have some very good news for you! As you plow through the upcoming chapters, you will encounter four forms used to anatomize the changes needed in operating pre-tax profit, operating cash flow, and employee compensation to meet the demands of the owners. They were *not* designed in a vacuum. Do not, I repeat, DO NOT become discouraged or disillusioned about the amount of tedium that you think you may have to face in preparing and using these forms! There is software commercially available today, at modest expense, that can be used with personal computers to perform all of the fifth-grade arithmetic needed to properly complete the columns and lines.

Yes, Incremental Gains can be computerized—easily and inexpensively. That means, of course, that you are excused from hustle-sapping tedium, and can play the "what if?" game with facility and ease to ensure that all of the feasible alternatives have been evaluated, *that all of the meaningful increments have been quantified!* So proceed now with a lighter heart.

Chapter 6

Measuring the Changes Needed in Operating Pre-Tax Profit

The key to success *tomorrow* is to so change the operating circumstances *today* that the generated operating results of *yesterday* will only be improved *tomorrow* and in the future. It is futile to expect or even look for changes in operating results if nothing has been done to change the operating circumstances which sired those results. It is as simple as that! And it also totally explains why CHANGE is, indeed, inevitable.

This is the first of three critical operating change measurement chapters. Here we anatomize the *changes needed in operating pre-tax profit* to produce the results demanded by the firms' owners and creditors. Generally, what I say here about the pattern of the analyses applies to the following two chapters equally as well. Try to gain a really good working knowledge and understanding of these three chapters. The rewards from that accomplishment will be long-lived and productive. The data, the "numbers" that you find at the interstices of this and the upcoming three anatomization figures, form the links in the chain of communication through the Total Compensation and Control and Reporting Systems.

Bear in mind when studying Chapters 6, 7, and 8 that the underlying purpose of the four figures is threefold. First, *Figures 3 thru 6 are the most useful and economical communication tools that you will ever use.* It is in the interstices of these figures that negotiation and finalization of levels of performance results will occur. Use the forms to focus attention and communication on only those action areas that contribute directly to performance improvement.

Second, the data finalized on these figures constitute the raw material of an outstanding Control and Reporting System! Adjectives and adverbs will simply not prevail. The numbers will tell the tale. Yet, in a way, given the unique crispness and impersonality of the data reported, even the Control and Reporting System serves to enhance the communication within the organization.

Third, the actual results, when compared to the planned results in the interstices, constitutes the essence of the formula for payment of incentive compensation. *Thus, Figure 3 is easily the most important form that your organization will ever complete—if, if* you're really trying to run your firm in a professional manner!

In a firm that has been in operation for several years, the planning for next year, if it's done at all, starts late in the third quarter, usually around August or September if the firm uses a calendar fiscal year.

Every fiscal autumn that time comes again when department heads, functional vice presidents, division presidents, and, yes, even group executives don their ballet slippers and tutus and begin the ritual of "Let's see how little I

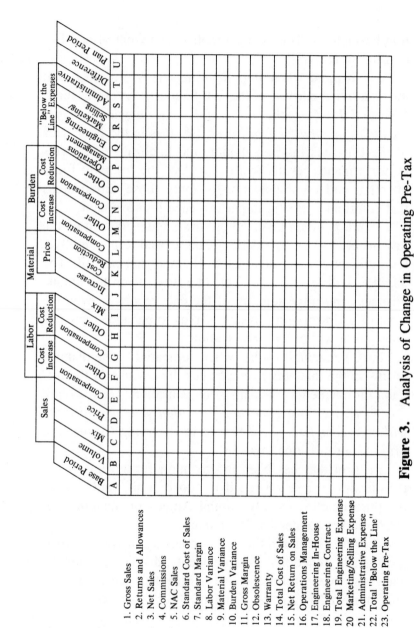

Figure 3. Analysis of Change in Operating Pre-Tax

126

will be held accountable for!" It's called BUDGETING, or Profit Planning, or the Search for Excellence!

Studies have been made, of course, of the cost of purchasing versus purchase cost and the cost of cost accounting, and so on. While I have not seen studies on the cost of preparing a budget, I would guess that it is substantial, particularly if performed in the time-honored sequence of present/review, re-present/re-review, re-re-present/re-re-review—ad nauseam, all part of playing the game of "hide and fudge factor."

Preoccupation with the sales line (or *any* line other than pre-tax) leads to excessive, unnecessary, and unproductive bookkeeping exercises in preparing the basic fundamental documents: income statement; balance sheet; cash (or funds) flow.

How does one cut through all the Mickey Mouse and get to the heart of the matter? How does one elevate the budgeting process from an accounting department add-on work task (ugh!) to an exercise of management challenge that results in personal accountability to quantified "stretch" objectives upon which meaningful, impersonal incentive compensation can be based? Got your attention? Read on.

First of all the "boss" (the guy/gal in the "corner office": the chairman, the CEO, or whatever title) sets the threshold of performance and the ground rules. Then, subordinates develop their plans/strategies to minimally reach the threshold in conformance with the ground rules. Shown below is a list of some examples of them for you to use if you don't already have any of your own. Now, as you read through them, don't waste my time or yours by playing the "what if" game—you know, where you read that the performance requirement is "so and so," and then you lean back and say, "Hell, I can think of a case that can be constructed to support (or destroy) that of any position." *You're not reading this book to try to win a debate with me.* You're reading it to see if there is a way to avoid most of the nonsensical waste of time and money usually incurred in budget preparation. Well, there is a way. And if you don't have enough creativity, knowledge-ability, and influence to effect favorable changes in your firm, stop reading right now. You will only be frustrated.

Some examples of sound, universally acceptable minimum performance thresholds are listed below in no particular order of priority:

- Selling price increases will at least keep pace with inflation.
- Selling price action will be based on "what the market will bear," not as markup from cost.
- Profitability will improve over prior period, whether measured as Return on Sales or, preferably, as Return on Investment.
- Cost reduction programs will at least offset effects of inflation and/or contractual obligations which will increase cost/expense.

Notice that they all have one thing in common: They all are addressed solely to pre-tax effect. *Not market share, not sales, not anything else!* Bankers and financial analysts have deep, abiding interest *only* in profit-per-share; they have no interest in "market-share-per-share" or "anything-else-per-share." Shareholders should also be similarly interested; too often they are not, but that's another book.

Because the cardinal interest and focus is at the pre-tax

line, it logically follows that the budget process should begin with an "Analysis of Changes in Operating Pre-Tax." Until that analysis and the consequent projection is accepted, it is pointless and a waste of precious time and money to prepare any of the detailed financials. It should be the first form used in budget preparation.

First of all, be mindful that even with the most thorough and complete utilization, most of the intersectional cells will be blanks. In other words, don't allow your subordinates to be overawed by the mere appearance of the form (of course, *you* won't be). This is *not* a "government" form, where it is required that all the blanks be filled in.

Second, note that it is *not* an accounting form. This form is aimed at communication at the management level. It provides a blend of traditional-accounting-system data and non-accounting-system data/treatment, such as population levels and the ground rule that parentheses *always* means *unfavorable* (all together now—hurray!—from those of us who always have trouble keeping it straight!).

Third, it is *not* a "magic" form. It is only *a* version of what you should refine or tailor to suit the needs of your particular firm. Nor will filling it out and filing it away result in achievement of objectives. It is, after all, only a tool. And how you, as the craftsman, *use* that tool will really determine what the end results will be.

THE COLUMNS

1. Effect of Sales on Pre-Tax

Columns B, C, and D present, respectively, the budgeted changes (both favorable and unfavorable) from the prior year in volume, mix, and price. Thus, direct measurable clarity is focused on what otherwise is, at best, a "fuzzy" number. Volume and mix projections can be interrogated back into the supporting plans for order intake, which, in turn, can be further traced into the supporting sales promotion and new product plans to ensure harmony and consistency in both timing and dollars.

Targeting a specific price effect provides managerial audit of the pricing program to ensure timing and adequacy of amount of increase, to ensure capture so that, in turn, the planned pre-tax contribution is achieved.

2. Effect of Manufacturing Cost on Pre-Tax

Columns E through O provide for display of specifics relative to budgeted behavior of the three prime cost elements: Labor; Material; and Burden. Labor covers Columns E, F, G, and H. The pattern of analysis for both Labor and Burden, as we shall see later, is the same; namely, first the identification of elements that increase cost, then identification of cost reduction goals to offset the cost increases. First the "bad news," then the "good news." For Labor analysis, both "compensation" and "other" are shown. Thus, inferences can be quantified relative to average wages paid and effect on efficiency (by cross-reference to Line 8, Labor Variance), insight is gained into the burden absorption base (cross-referencing compensation with Line 10, Burden Variance), labor efficiency levels are identified earlier, and so on. Similarly, the aggressiveness of planned cost reduction is more visible through study of Columns

G and H, both in absolute terms and in comparative or relative terms by cross-reference to population percent changes, which are affected by cost reduction, and so on.

The key determinants of Material Cost are Mix (Column I) and Price (Columns J and K). In each of these instances, quantified projections are required to show both the unfavorable and the favorable budgeted performances.

Burden Cost (Columns L through O) is analyzed again from both the Increases and the Cost Reduction viewpoints, again relating compensation levels to expense levels. Columns M and O, Other Expenses, are not meant to mean "miscellaneous"; they include all expenses not directly related to population. The numbers can be quite large.

3. Effect of "Below the Line" Expenses on Pre-Tax

Columns P through S present both the favorable and the unfavorable effects on planned performance. In each case, population levels must be related to dollar expense levels for managerial "reasonability testing."

Column T is used to display the summed changes recorded in Columns B through S. Column U is derived by combining Columns A and T.

THE LINES

Now let's proceed line by line down the Income Statement. Lines 1 through 5 deal exclusively with Sales. Returns and Allowances, and Commissions are deducted from Gross

Sales to arrive at Net After Commission (NAC) Sales. They interface essentially with Columns B, C, and D.

Lines 6 through 10 evaluate Cost of Goods Sold so that, by subtraction, the Gross Margin, Line 11, is generated. Figure 4 is designed to accommodate a standard cost system. If you use another costing method, merely substitute the appropriate lines. Inferences drawn from intersectional entries on the Variance lines (8, 9, and 10) are particularly useful. Insight into the planned changes, for example, in labor efficiency, can be gained by study of the entries in the Labor Variance–Compensation (or Line 8–Column G) intersection.

Given steady or rising volume (Column B), decreases in population should improve Labor Variance, or at least reduce the adverse effect of increased wages (Column E).

Line 11, Gross Margin, is sometimes called Factory Profit. To obtain Total Cost of Sales (or Cost of Goods Sold), provision for Obsolescence (Line 12) and Warranty (Line 13) costs are subtracted from Gross Margin (Line 11).

The Net Return on Sales (Line 15) shows the gross profit available to cover operating expenses and operating pretax.

Lines 16 through 21 show planned behavior of the Below the Line expenses. Line 16, Operations Management, assumes that production control/scheduling, purchasing, industrial or manufacturing engineering, and so on are treated as period or line item expenses. This simply means that they are not included in the burden pool and thus are not incorporated into inventory via burden absorption. This is probably the most conservative treatment. It keeps these costs off the balance sheet and retains them in the income statement. It tends to reduce reported operating pre-tax, particularly if volume is sufficiently high to permit overabsorption.

Lines 17 and 18 provide means to analyze Engineering Expense from both the In-House and Contract viewpoints. Selling Expense (Line 20) includes marketing, advertising, promotion, shows, conventions, and so on, as well as direct selling expenses.

Administrative Expense (Line 21) includes the usual assortment of accounting, finance, administrative, accrual, interest, and other expenses. Line 22 (Total "Below the Line") is the sum of Lines 16 through 21 and is subtracted from Line 15 (Net Return on Sales) to arrive, finally, at Operating Pre-Tax, Line 23.

Okay, now that you and Figure 3 have become good friends, let's proceed to learn how we can best control, plan, and achieve cash flow objectives.

Chapter 7

Measuring the Changes Needed in Operating Cash Flow

In this chapter, I examine what, in many cases, is even more important than the subject of Chapter 6, namely, the analysis of the changes needed in operating pre-tax profit. Here I define each and every planned change in the operating cash flow and identify the cognizant functional responsibility for achievement of that change; that is, we pinpoint *who* is on the hook for *how much* and *when* the firm's cash flow must be changed.

THE COLUMNS

Again, I'm in the enviable position of dispelling mystery and puzzlement. There are only eight ways that operating cash flow can be affected—for good or otherwise (see Figure 4). Those eight ways are captured in the eight columns, B through I. Just as you saw in Chapter 6 and as you will see in Chapter 8, the first column, A, displays, as always, the most likely results that will eventuate if no

	Base Period	Volume	Mix	Price Increase	Price Decrease	Cost/Expense Increase	Cost/Expense Decrease	Terms	Acct'g Change	Other	Diff.	Plan Period
	A	B	C	D	E	F	G	H	I	J	K	L
Income Statement												
1. Returns & Allowances												
2. Net Sales												
3. Commissions												
4. Material												
5. Labor												
6. Burden												
7. Warranty/Field Service												
8. Operations Management												
9. Engineering: In-House												
10. Engineering: Contract												
11. Marketing/Selling Expense												
12. Finance/Accounting Changes												
13. Depreciation												
14. Other Noncash Changes												
Balance Sheet												
15. Net Receivables: $		///		///	///	///	///		///	///		
16. Net Receivables: DSO		///		///	///	///	///		///	///		
17. Inventory												
18. Prepaid Expenses												
19. Accounts Payable: $		///		///	///	///	///		///	///		
20. Accounts Payable: DPO		///		///	///	///	///		///	///		
21. Accruals												
22. Capital Expenditures												
23. Total $												

Figure 4. Analysis of Change in Operating Cash Flow

135

significant operational changes are made—that is, it shows the run-rate forecast.

Column K, Difference, "totals" algebraically the net results of the "puts and takes," the additions and subtractions that were posted in the interim columns.

Column B, then, shows the entries which relate to changes in the physical volume of sales, whether favorable or otherwise. The entries in Column C reflect the changes in sales revenue due to changes in product mix. The results of decisions related to product pruning and so on are captured also in Column C. Columns D and E show the effect of planned change in selling price.

The effect of planned cost and expense reductions (or, heaven forbid, increases), are captured in Columns F and G.*

The planned changes in payment Terms, whether related to Purchases or to Sales, are shown in Column H. Thus, planned changes, for instance, in lengthening payables will be shown at the intersection of Column H and Line 4, Material.

Column I shows any planned change due to changes in accounting procedure or treatment. The greatest impact here occurs, generally, because of changes or expected changes in the various tax laws.

Any "Other" changes are shown in Column J. The algebraic, horizontal sum of the changes posted in Columns B thru J is shown in Column K. Thus, line by line, the amount shown in Column A plus/minus the total of the

---

* For a complete discussion of "The Crucial Difference Between Costs and Expenses," pages 123–126 of _THE_ _Turnaround Manager's Handbook_, The Free Press, 1985. It will be well worth your while.

changes in Columns B thru J is shown in the difference, Column K.

In summary, Column A, plus/minus Column K, equals Column L. Note again that *any time period can be selected by computation of the Increment Differences, so long as the same period is used for all of the columns.*

THE LINES

Lines 1, 2, and 3 relate to changes in Sales Revenue. Of particular importance is an increase in selling price. Such increases have uniquely significant and favorable effect on cash flow: namely, they are directly dollar for dollar, additive to the favorable cash flow to the owners. Generally, you will enter performance objectives in Columns B thru E.

Lines 4 through 14 deal with *cash expenditures* related to the Operating Profit and Loss Statement, whereas, Lines 1 through 3 focused on *cash revenue sources* on the Operating Profit and Loss Statement. Performance objectives will generally be entered in many of the columns, particularly if there are significant changes planned in sales volume, operating run-rate, or inventory.

Thus, the amounts entered in the interstices of Columns A through L and Lines 1 through 14 can be (and should be) directly traced and related to the intersticial amounts entered in Figure 3. Analysis of Changes in Operating Pre-Tax Profit.

Lines 15 through 22 house the planned changes to selected Balance Sheet items. The pattern of the posted change performance objectives should, generally, directly mirror the pattern of change planned for sales volume and/or operating run-rate. That is, if volume or plant activity is planned to increase, one would expect corresponding, but slightly less than, proportional increases in Receivables and Inventory.

Lines 16 and 20 warrant particular attention. The entries made are *not* dollar amounts. They are, respectively, the equivalent number of days of sales volume that are yet uncollected receivables (Days Sales Outstanding, or DSO) and the equivalent number of days of purchase volume that are yet unpaid payables (Days Purchases Outstanding, or DPO). At the risk of oversimplification, these two performance indicators tell us who is financing whom. If DSO rises, it says that we are financing our customers. If, on the other hand, DPO rises, it means that our vendors are financing us. An increasing DPO is always better.

Line 22 is included here principally to make sure that you take Capital Expenditures into account. In many firms, this amount is not usually a dominant factor. Feel free to modify this figure, of course, to more closely tailor it to your firm's needs. You may want to add a line—for example, New Product Development, or Research and Development—to keep closer track of a commonly used tax deduction.

Finally, a gentle reminder that posting the performance objective entries in this figure, as also in Figures 4, 6, and 7, is *only* the beginning. These are inputs into both the Control and Reporting Systems, and the Compensation System as shown in Figure 2, Practicing Management by Incremental Gains.

Chapter 8

Measuring the Changes Needed in Employee Compensation Costs/Expenses

You will find that Figure 5, Analysis of Change in Employee Compensation Cost/Expense, is, if not *the* most valuable, then certainly one of the most valuable management control and planning documents that you have ever used or ever will use. Not only does this form clearly and succinctly reveal the assignable and controllable units of some 30–40 percent of your firm's entire operating pre-tax profit, it also reveals where some 30–40 percent of your firm's CASH expenditures goes! Thus, consistent with my No-Nonsense "Pareto" system of priorities, this analysis gives you all the basic management tools for more effective administration, planning, and control for the largest component of both your firm's operating pre-tax profit *and* cash flow!

Further, the format itself of Figure 5 provides the basis for personal accountability, for objective setting, for "sanity test" checking against Figures 3 and 4 and so on. Note

	Base Period	Volume	Mix	Compensation		Other	Diff.	Plan Period
				Increase	Decrease			
	A	B	C	D	E	F	G	H
($000 where appropriate)								
Labor 1. Direct Compensation								
2. Indirect Compensation								
3. Population				XX	XX			
4. Hourly Direct Compensation								
5. Hourly Indirect Compensation								
Burden 6. Hourly Population				XX	XX			
7. Salary Direct Compensation								
8. Salary Indirect Compensation								
9. Salary Population				XX	XX			
10. Hourly Direct Compensation								
11. Hourly Indirect Compensation								
Warranty Field Service 12. Hourly Population				XX	XX			
13. Salary Direct Compensation								
14. Salary Indirect Compensation								
15. Salary Population				XX	XX			
16. Hourly Direct Compensation								
17. Hourly Indirect Compensation								
Operations Mgmnt 18. Hourly Population				XX	XX			
19. Salary Direct Compensation								
20. Salary Indirect Compensation								
21. Salary Population				XX	XX			
22. Hourly Direct Compensation								
23. Hourly Indirect Compensation								
Engineering 24. Hourly Population				XX	XX			
25. Salary Direct Compensation								
26. Salary Indirect Compensation								
27. Salary Population				XX	XX			
28. Hourly Direct Compensation								
29. Hourly Indirect Compensation								
Selling Marketing 30. Hourly Population				XX	XX			
31. Salary Direct Compensation								
32. Salary Indirect Compensation								
33. Salary Population				XX	XX			
34. Hourly Direct Compensation								
35. Hourly Indirect Compensation								
Finance Admin. 36. Hourly Population				XX	XX			
37. Salary Direct Compensation								
38. Salary Indirect Compensation								
39. Salary Population				XX	XX			
40. Hourly Direct Compensation								
41. Hourly Indirect Compensation								
Totals 42. Hourly Population				XX	XX			
43. Salary Direct Compensation								
44. Salary Indirect Compensation								
45. Salary Population				XX	XX			

Figure 5. Analysis of Change in Employee Compensation Cost/Expense

	Base Period	Diff.	Plan Period
($000 where appropriate)	A	B	C
1. Total Hourly Direct Compensation			
2. Total Salary Direct Compensation			
3. Total Direct Compensation			
4. Total Hourly Indirect Compensation			
5. Total Salary Indirect Compensation			
6. Total Indirect Compensation			
7. Total Hourly Compensation			
8. Total Salary Compensation			
9. Total Compensation			
10. Total Hourly Population			
11. Total Salary Population			
12. Total Population			
13. Average Hourly Direct Compensation			
14. Average Hourly Indirect Compensation			
15. Average Hourly Total Compensation			
16. Average Salary Direct Compensation			
17. Average Salary Indirect Comepnsation			
18. Average Salary Total Comepnsation			
19. Total Direct Compensation/Net Sales			
20. Total Indirect Compensation/Net Sales			
21. Total Compensation/Net Sales			

Figure 6. Employee Compensation Cost/Expense Action Summary

that provision is made for display of population data so that here and in Figure 6, Employee Compensation Cost/ Expense Action Summary, both the preparer and the reviewer can easily perform reasonability tests to ensure exclusion and avoidance of gross errors in the final array of performance objectives in the firm's Profit Plan.

An example of one of the many interrelated insights that more strongly legitimizes the firm's total Profit Plan is shown below. If, say, "Sales Volume" shows increases in pre-tax (Figure 3) and cash flow (Figure 4), then there should be a corresponding increase in Figure 5 on Line 3, Labor Population, in Column B, Volume.

Another example: If, say, Mix shows increases in pre-tax (Figure 3) and cash flow (Figure 4) because of a new, higher technological content product, then increases in Field Service/Warranty Population and Compensation (Lines 10–15) should be proportionately shown.

Figure 6, in addition to presenting a summary of the detail in Figure 5, also contains "Average" Compensation data (Lines 13–18), which are very useful for historical comparisons as well as for sanity checking of the planned changes. And, finally, Lines 19–21 display three of the probably most important productivity measures that your firm will ever use. If, for instance, the ratios increase continually year after year, your firm is in growingly deep trouble. The idea is to at least keep the ratio value constant and, at best, to be able to chart their behavior as a gently downward sloping curve.

Chapter 9

Making the Changes Happen!

Morale is always higher among those workers who meet the *high demands made upon them—and are shown appreciation for meeting them*—than among a group that works under sloppy supervision with low or no standards set for workers' performance.

This chapter boasts an ambitious title indeed! After all, "Making the Changes Happen!" is another way of saying Execution Implementation, Getting it done! And we all know that preparation and pursuit are one thing, akin to the check that's "in the mail." But having that check "in the bank" is quite another matter altogether. *You haven't got it until you've got it.* This chapter, then, deals with the motivation of individuals, of management personnel in a for-profit business context.

THE ELEMENTS OF MOTIVATION

As I consistently did in earlier chapters, I will first define the basic terms that I will address and use in this especially important chapter.

Motivation: A need or desire that causes a person to take
    some action.
Motive: An emotion or desire operating on a person's
    will and, thereby, causing it, in turn, to generate action.
Incentive: This applies to an external inducement (as
    an expected reward) inciting one to action.

While a great deal of (sometimes) arcane literature has
already been inflicted on the reading management public,
this slight addition will provide disproportionately more
light than load. The nature and anatomy of motivation is
really not all that mysterious—at least so far as it applies
to more than 95 percent of management personnel. That's
why "professional" or academic dissertations are so
lengthy, by the way. It takes disproportionately far more
time and paper to adequately discuss the extensive variety
of extraordinary cases which occur in the remaining 0–5
percent. This should not be a surprise. Pareto's Law, you
know, operates equally effectively throughout the real world
(at least 95 percent of the time). So, in keeping with my
no-nonsense approach, let's just ignore those fascinating,
but rarely encountered myriad complications, shall we, and
just concentrate on the more than 95 percent who already
either are or want to be operating management personnel.

There are really only eight principal, crucial factors that
you have to take into account if you are seriously trying
to create and/or enhance enduringly higher levels of management motivation. Not only is the number of factors
small and manageable, but this book provides you with
all the theoretical *and* practical information you will need
to successfully obtain the improvement you seek. The eight

Motivation Factors are discussed below and are *presented from the viewpoint of the employee.* You're going to put yourself in the shoes of the subordinate. You will cite your demands and ask your questions as if you were the embodiment of one of the more than 95 percent of management personnel and those who so aspire.

While I haven't seen this approach used elsewhere in management literature, it is, nonetheless, a most effective technique. Look on it as a sales situation. The "order" we're after is for the employee/manager to become (more) motivated. *The best, time-tested, proven sales technique is to solve the customer's problem more effectively and completely than any other alternative that he has.* So what better way to begin our program to improve motivation than to define, measure, and otherwise more completely understand the employee/manager's "problems" that hinder or even preclude improvement of motivation? What are the key "hot buttons" that can turn him on? We're going to save a lot of your time and mine by answering, exclusively, only those really few burning questions/demands that each of us asks when facing the work environment.

MF 1: Treat Me as an Individual!

Look at *me!* Talk to *me!* Listen to *me!*

While I am indeed a member of a group, I am a unique member. There is no other member precisely like me. Don't apply a simplistic label and then consign me to a confining pigeonhole.

I *can* contribute! I want to contribute. I want to do a good job. I want to be proud of what I do. I want to feel important, that I'm trusted and relied upon. I may not always have great ideas, but I do have some. I'm basically an honest person. I look forward to doing a fair day's work for a fair day's pay. I'm loyal—maybe not so much to "the company," but certainly to the people with whom I work.

When you fail to distinguish *me* from the "others," you turn me off and not only destroy whatever level of motivation I may have, you transform me into your adversary.

MF 2: What is Expected of Me?

I cannot even begin to feel that I'm doing a good job until I clearly know what it is you want me to do. That's not too much to ask and it *is* vitally important for my motivation that I feel as though I'm doing a good job. I look to you to explain and identify for me precisely what the levels of acceptable performance are. After all, if you left it up to me (and every other subordinate) the firm would certainly be posting suboptimal results and very likely would be in Chapter 11. There simply must be leadership.

Oh, sure, I've got a pretty good basic idea of what I'm supposed to do. If, for instance, I'm a Sales Manager, then I know my job will deal largely with obtaining orders and satisfying customers. But how much of an improvement in sales volume or sales price or product mix, etc., do you expect me to generate? And how soon? When do you expect these improvements to be posted on our books of account?

It's very important that both of us have a very good idea of what is expected of me. It's impossible for me to be an expert marksman if I don't know where the bull's-eye is.

MF 3: How Can I Progress in the Organization?

I'm going to try very hard. I'm going to work smart. I'm determined to succeed. I'm improving my skills with ongoing education and training. I'm serious about my career.

What, then, are the upward avenues, ways, career paths, and so on that I can realistically expect to travel? How can I improve my lot? And I want to know specifically, not just be told generalized platitudes. So keep the oratorical rhetoric to yourself, thank you, and level with me. The more avenues, paths, and so on that I can perceive, depend on, observe, inspect, ponder, and pursue, the greater will be my motivation to progress.

MF 4: If I Perform Well, How Will I Be Rewarded?

Let's say there are the reporting procedures in place such that you and I are convinced that I did, in fact, perform well. What I want to know, precisely, is how will I be rewarded?

What is the difference in reward, if there is any, between whether I perform merely adequately or whether I perform in a clearly outstanding manner? What does the reward consist of? Money? A gold watch? A letter of commendation? A lunch? What? How much?

The most important point here ties back to Motivation Factor 1. Namely, if I perform well, I want to be commensurately rewarded regardless and irrespective of (a) how other employees may have performed, and (b) the "so-called" profit reported by the firm, division, or whatever the name of the organization of which I am a member. *I want my competence to be judged solely and exclusively on my performance, not on any other external, extraneous factors.* Did I, or did I not meet/exceed the performance objectives that we agreed on? That's the *only* issue!

It's very important that I know the answers to these questions *before* I take on the obligation to perform. I really don't want any surprises after I've busted my tail. The greater the rewards, the greater will be my motivation to meet/exceed them. The less I know about reward expectations, the less I will be motivated to perform well.

MF 5: If I Perform Well, When Will I Be Rewarded?

As far as ordinary compensation is concerned, how often will my performance be reviewed for the purpose of possibly awarding an increase? How long and how continuously must I perform well to earn an increase?

With regard to incentive compensation, how long will I have to wait to get the money? Until the books are "closed"? Until the firm has been audited? Until after the Annual Report is published? When?

The sooner, after performance of results, I get my money, the more I will be motivated to achieve the necessary results. On the other hand, the longer I have to wait, the less interested I become about the whole thing.

MF 6: If (Unthinkable) I Fail to Perform as Expected, How Will I Be Treated?

Just what will happen if, for some reason or another, I fail to achieve the expected levels of performance or objectives? The first time? Subsequently? How much and what kind of help, assistance, guidance, and so on can I expect to receive? From whom? Just how much consideration will be given to forces and circumstances beyond my control? Is there an established, published procedure that I can look to and rely on? How do I know I'll be treated fairly, with dignity?

Clearly, the greater my confidence that I will be treated as a professional, with focus on my performance and not on my personality, the higher will be the level of my motivation. Once again, not surprisingly, the converse is true. Namely, the greater the uncertainty of my unplanned fate the less likely it is that I will seek greater responsibility, vulnerability, visibility, and so on. In short, the less will be my desire, my motivation to act.

MF 7: I Want to Keep Track, by Myself, of How I'm Doing!

I know that it is almost always the case that performance only rarely occurs all at once. Progress toward a goal or objective almost always occurs step-by-step, day by day, etc. As I put forth effort and apply myself, I want to know how I'm doing along the way. No sense letting too much time get wasted if I'm off-track, right? Of course!

Not only do I want to know how I'm doing, I want the measurement of my progress to be such that (a) it is an acceptable gauge to all of my superiors, and (b) I can perform the calculations myself. The more those two characteristics prevail, the greater the legitimacy of my personal record of how I'm doing. And that, in turn, increases my interest, enthusiasm and motivation. Conversely, the less I am in control of keeping track of my interim progress, the less I become personally identified not only with progress toward the objectives, but with the objectives themselves.

MF 8: Where Do I Stand in Relation to My Peers?

Much, much more than mere idle curiosity lies behind this pressing question. I want to know how my performance record compares to those of my peers to ensure that the record is clear to everyone as to who is pulling their weight and who is not. The greater the quantitativeness of the comparison, the less likely it will be that subjective evaluations, criticisms, and excuses will prevail. In short, the less likely it will be that "office politics" will flourish.

And I do not want to be involved or affected by "politicking." It's just as important to *me* that they know how *I'm* doing as it is for *me* to know how *they're doing*. Open and aboveboard measurement and publication of everyone's performance helps us focus on all that really matters: performance results!

The lesser the role that politics plays in the organization, the greater the importance placed upon individual, measurable performance. In turn, then, my level and intensity of motivation rise and fall correspondingly.

If those, then, are the foundational Motivation Factors, what are the techniques or procedures that support and sustain them? They are a blend of two basic management systems: a Control and Reporting System, and a comprehensive Compensation and Performance Evaluation System. The former enables management to exercise Control in an effective, equitable, and consistent manner. The latter fosters and promotes Employee Motivation. At first blush, it might seem that this is a strange, to say the least, combination. Upon closer examination, however, it is quite clear that the two systems, if professionally managed of course, constitute a genuine and powerful symbiosis. Webster tells us that a symbiosis is "the intimate living together of two dissimilar [systems] in a mutually beneficial relationship." Let's explore these two systems first and then see how they synergistically merge to constitute effective fulfillment of all eight Motivation Factors.

CONTROL AND REPORTING
—AN OVERVIEW

Control and Reporting are commonly grouped together. That's rather curious since "Reporting" is an activity traditionally defined or described in terms of formatted hard-copy reports and the procedures (or rules) by which the reports are prepared. "Control," on the other hand, is really more of an attitude . . . It reflects the personality, if you will, of the organization. One traditionally speaks of loose or tight control. The degree of control often connotes the relative ease or difficulty with which approval is obtained to commit resources to a proposed course of action.

The two systems are not unrelated, however. It usually works this way. The owners (or their designates) set the pace. That is, they decide, whether purposefully or by default, what the flavor, intensity, scope, and application of Control shall be in their firm. The formulation and expression of the Control "attitude" always comes first and it always proceeds from the top down. Once the owners (or their designates) make clear, either explicitly or, more usually, implicitly what "control" will mean to that particular organization at that particular time, the reporting requirements necessary to meet the implementational needs of that control level become clear.

Control and Reporting, and Compensation, are substitute labels for, respectively, Nonfinancial Motivation and Financial Motivation, see Figure 7. Note that the Nonfinancial elements are presented first. This is not by accident. Since Reporting is an outgrowth and function of Control, it is presented after Control. And since Control is the expressed ownership attitude, the owners' demands, desires come first (Remember? Sloma's Golden Rule!) Finally, it is the result of decisions about the Reporting System upon which Compensation administration is dependent. Thus, the "proper

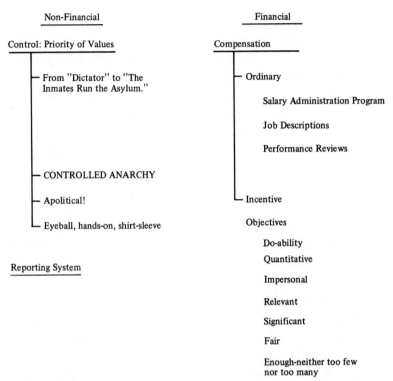

Figure 7. The Anatomy of Management Motivation

sequence'' is as shown: Control, Reporting, Compensation.

The range of type or nature of Control is wide indeed. While it varies over time within every organization, we will not consider those complications in this book. Rather, our viewpoint is looking forward through time with the aim of maximizing the financial return on the shareholders' investment. The Control exercised always emulates Style, and thus cases within the full gamut from ''Dictator'' to

"Chaos," where the "inmates run the asylum," can and do occur in the real world. As each owner or owner group makes trade-off decisions between financial and psychic return on investment, the effect of that decision locates a particular position within the Control/Style spectrum.

There is, thankfully, only one location on the spectrum where the maximization of the financial return on investment is generated. That point on the Control/Style spectrum can best be defined as "Controlled Anarchy." The notion is that the fundamental, key financial and accounting procedures are in place such that (a) major expenditures, policy initiations, and decisions are routed through appropriate approval levels, and (b) each individual management/key person is motivated to pursue, unfettered, his own selfish goals and objectives.

If the definition of that Control/Style were forced into only one word, that word would be "apolitical." That is to say, an effective Control System is one which is devoid of the debilitating and devastating effect of "office politics." Among its other salient characteristics are two critical hallmarks of success. The first, cogently put, is: *Concentrate all attention on results—waste no significant amount of time on effort*. The inherent value of this approach is that it precludes search for a goat. It tends to keep everyone's eye on performance rather than on personality.

The second characteristic stretches for anthropomorphic analogy. It is generally accepted that, somehow, "feet on the ground," "eyeball," "hands-on," "nose to the grindstone," and "shirt-sleeve" management is, somehow, more effective. And as I can attest, after more than twenty years of observation, that proves to be almost universally the case!

THE ANATOMY OF CONTROL

The essence of Managing by Incremental Gain, and the basis of Control, can be summarized in just three words:

Anatomize: Then Synthesize

The anatomization process is certainly as critical to success as the synthesization. The essense of anatomization is the notion of the "increment." What does Webster say to us about it? An "increment" is: "the action or process of increasing especially in quantity or value . . . something gained or added . . . *one of a series of regular consecutive additions . . . the amount of positive or negative change in the value of one or more of a set of variables*" (emphasis added).

To the extent that a firm's organization produces satisfactory results, it is practicing the principle of "anatomize: then synthesize." In fact, MRPII, JIT, Quality Circles, Zero Defects, Theory Z (and X and Y, too, for that matter), and all versions of the "One-Minute" magic fluff—*all* will fail and even be counterproductive if they are not incrementally quantified, planned, and controlled!

Steps 1, 2, 3, 4, and 6 below describe the anatomization activity; Steps 5, 7, and 8 describe the synthesization activity. Let's walk through it with a little detail.

Step 1: Quantify the Demands
of the Owners/Creditors

What are the results that the owners/creditors demand to see in the future? Try to look no further out than one year. A quarterly pattern is very helpful if you can get it. Refresh yourself, if need be, with our discussion in Chapter 2 of what owners really want.

Step 2: Quantify the Run-Rate Forecast

Based on the financial and operational records thus far, what will results likely be in the future? Of course, match the same time period to that used by the owners/creditors. The basic notion is that no new action of significance would be initiated or executed in the interim. *We are trying to quantify what the future will most likely be if nothing new is done; if we continue only at our present run-rates.*

Step 3: Cite and Quantify
the Performance Differences

This step looks (and is) deceptively simple. What we're trying to do is ascertain where and how big the differences are between the owners' demands and the run-rate forecast.

Step 4: Quantify Specific Functional Differences

As a result of Step 3, we might be able to identify differences which are neatly and exclusively related to a single function in the organization. For instance, a requirement for an increase in Order Intake clearly falls in the purview of the Marketing/Sales function of the firm. And so on.

Step 5: Personal Assignment to Formulate Action Plans

Negotiate the assignment personally with the functional manager to document an Action Plan which, if reasonably well executed, will likely yield results at least equal to 105 percent of the earlier measured difference between the owners' demands and the run-rate forecast—the performance "gap."

Almost without exception, only a small part of the total performance difference can be accounted for using Steps 4 and 5. It will almost always be necessary to proceed through Steps 6 and 7 because that will be the only way the entire performance difference or gap can be successfully bridged. Operational performance gaps rarely fall entirely within a single function; they almost always overlap functions.

Step 6: Present Differences to the Functional Managers

Those who are respectively responsible for the major functions of the firm (sales, production, engineering, finance, and so on) and the president/general manager are often collectively termed the "Executive Committee." Keeping in mind the adage that "No one will ever learn anything until they realize that they have a problem," makes the Executive Committee aware, in agonizing and excruciating detail, of the nature, extent, and scope of the performance gap if the interest of the owners is to be retained.

Step 7: Personal Assignment to Prepare Functional Action Plans

Once the magnitude and details of the total performance gap have been quantified *and* communicated, each of the firm's functional managers should be charged with the responsibility to develop and present specific action plans aimed at bridging that performance gap. Unless there are uniquely relevant functional performance gaps (see Steps 4 and 5), the functional managers should be given only the general assignment to improve operating pre-tax and cash flow as much as possible.

The extent of each of the functional improvement requirements cannot really be ascertained until the sum of all the functional contributions to improvement is compared to the total performance gap. If you give specific targets prematurely, you run two unnecessary risks. First, you may cite an amount and/or time frame that is unrealistically aggressive or optimistic. As the functional managers try to formulate action plans to achieve those objectives, frustration will quickly turn to anxiety and alienation. The objectives will have become "your" objectives, *not* theirs! There will be no commitment. Don't play God.

On the other hand, you may define too soft an objective:

too low an amount and/or a date too far in the future. In that case, the functional managers will not be challenged or stretched. They will receive fortuitous or windfall incentive compensation. Complicating things further, soft targets are never uniformly set over all functions. Those who do not receive them will perceive those who do as "favored" and you as unfair. In summary, if you set objectives prematurely, it is very likely that you will upset the entire management group; some will not be challenged because they will be overwhelmed while others will not be challenged because they are underwhelmed and thereby become the targets of discontent of the overwhelmed. It is far more effective to carefully keep the onus on each of the subordinates to do "their very best," to come up with the biggest pledge that they can, to give till it hurts.

Step 8: Does the Sum of the Functional Action Plans Exceed the Total Performance Difference?

This is the key question, the key step. *The sum of the planned functional improvements must somewhat exceed the measured total performance gap.* We all live in an imperfect world, after all. Execution of management action plans is always less than perfect. So the aim had better be sufficiently above the bull's-eye to allow for the real world trajectory drop.

It is worthy of special note that Steps 3 through 8 provide professionally high levels of participation and communication. As the focus of review and evaluation rises and falls through levels in the organization, there can be no excuse for failure of individual participation. The more the ''yo-yo'' syndrome is practiced, the greater will be the degree of knowledgeability and commitment of each individual manager.

Step 9: Document Incentive Compensation Program

Because of the exhaustive and rigorous reviews that you and your staff have conducted, you are finally convinced that each of the functional management teams has been stretched and that the sum of their individual commitments sufficiently exceed the total performance gap which was quantified in Step 3. *Documentation of the Incentive Compensation Program is facilitated by the format and the formalization of each individual's performance objectives.* The elements and construction of an Incentive Compensation Program are discussed in detail later in this chapter. However, let's touch on enough highlights here to make sure this chapter is understood. There should be no cap or ceiling on the amount of incentive compensation that can be earned. The individual should have maximum practical control over his performance commitment. The participant should be able to track his own progress. The performance objective and the results of actual performance should be both measurable and independently verifiable.

A brief note about the relationship of Job Descriptions and Incentive Compensation Programs. *The purpose of the Job Description is to so define the everyday activity of an individual such that a commensurate and appropriate salary level can be derived which is, at once, equitable to that individual and, comparatively, to other individuals in the organization.* The Job Description is the cornerstone document of any Salary Administration Program. It should provide sufficient data to support salary levels (and related ranges) which are competitively attractive in the relevant labor market.

Incentive Compensation, on the other hand, is essentially a motivational tool. What you're trying to do is to get that individual to stretch, to grow, to give it that extra "something," to work harder, to work smarter, and so on. And to the extent that the individual performs—that is, gets desired results—he earns additional significant compensation.

It does, after all, take hard work to meet a demanding performance gap. Good intentions and/or strong efforts simply will not substitute for results. To the extent that harder work/tougher results are expected, the individual should receive proportionately additional pay. I cannot imagine a successful manager who is indifferent to earning more and more money unless he subscribes to Henny Youngman's view: "I've got all the money I'll ever need—if I die by four o'clock."

Step 10: Present Action Plans and Incentive Compensation Program to Owners/Creditors

In this step, you present all of the plans, commitments, and objectives from each of your participant/managers. Your aim is to convince/persuade the owners and/or creditors that their performance demands will indeed very likely be met.

You will also present the reporting and control procedures and techniques that you will employ to monitor interim progress. Your aim here is to sufficiently assure the owners/creditors that the entire effort is in good hands and to please let us operating guys just do our thing, already.

Step 11: Begin Execution

Because you have incorporated all the principles, wisdom, common sense, and spirit, as well as the letter of the Incremental Gains concept, you will be given instantaneous and hearty approval to proceed.

THE EIGHT ELEMENTS OF REPORTING

Of course, if you really scour the shelves of management literature, you will probably find many more so-called Elements of Reporting than I present below. But following the pattern established earlier with regard to motivation, I have gleaned the essentials and commonplace from the trivia and rare. Again, *more than 95 percent of the time, incorporation of these elements will achieve more than 95 percent success.*

RE 1: Management Reports: Not Accounting Reports

The reports should serve, principally, the needs of management, not the accountants. And what are some of the differences? The essential difference is that the management report should be designed to save management's precious time. It should be easy to read, convey as much information (not merely data) as possible per square inch, highlight what the management is interested in, needn't neatly cross-foot and down-foot, incorporate data from outside of the accounting system, and so on.

The key point is that the reports really should be different from the reams of reports traditionally prepared and distributed. Because they are intended for motivation and control of people, it is not surprising that they should differ significantly from those reports whose aim is to document transactions in a manner consistent with generally accepted accounting standards and principles.

In short, they should inform, communicate, and provide quantitative insights on which qualitative judgments and assessments can be made.

RE 2: Generate Questions/Facilitate Quantitative Answers

There are only two functional questions that ever need be addressed in the design of management reports! The first is: Did we perform better than we planned? If we did, the follow-on questions and interest should focus only on how even greater improvement can be obtained.

The second is: Did we perform worse than we planned? If that, unfortunately, is the case, then the follow-on questions and interest should focus exclusively on identi-fication of specific ways that the shortfall can be recouped and performance put back on-track as soon as possible.

RE 3: Comparisons, Comparisons, Comparisons. . .

Meaningful questions can only come from rigorous, relative, pertinent, significant, timely, and quantitative comparisons. The essence of an effective, useful management report is a combination of comparisons and the proper presentation of the results of those comparisons.

Just a few specifics which warrant special attention. First, be sure to always show the "percent difference" for all critical comparisons. It would be of even more help if the "percent difference" column were sorted in either descending or ascending sequence, depending on the nature of the numerators and denominators (see RE 4 below). Second, and *this is really important*, be sure your reporting system design includes comparative data for *all* of the objectives identified in the Incentive Compensation Program. Too often, I have seen situations where the Reporting System and the Incentive Compensation Program were badly out of sync. The net result was as counterproductive and ineffective as it was predictable!

RE 4: Forget General Ledger Account Numbers!

At least forget about them as far as using them for sequence control fields. Recall that we're trying to prepare a "management" report. So, then, look to the "amount" field or the "percent difference" field as the proper, effective sequence control. For instance, an Order Backlog Report is much more useful to management if the customers are listed in descending sequence of amount ordered than if they are listed in customer number or alphabetic sequence.

RE 5: Always Present the Bad News ASAP!

Professionally managed football teams and for-profit businesses *always* solidify the defense before they begin to take chances on the offense! Take those steps which *ensure* that you'll be in business tomorrow before you even begin to plan tomorrow's new product, new market, or new business. Sound advice? You bet! So what are the implications for our Reporting System?

Well, to put it as briefly as I can, always sort the results of the data comparisons in such a manner that *the worst of the bad news always tops the list.* That way, the manager/reader knows that there will never be any alligators waiting in the weeds on page 126—or 345.

RE 6: Stay as Close as You Can to the "Real World"

As you will learn in detail later, Incentive Compensation Program objectives are always more effective if they are measured by physical, real-world parameters rather than (only) by data bubbled up through the accounting system. I don't know, but somehow it just seems more believable, tangible, and reliable to talk about the number of hours that a work station is in operation than it is to talk about a scalar percentage change in an accrual provision.

So, as you design the Reporting System, make sure you incorporate the necessary (as many as you can) valid data flows from non-accounting-system sources.

RE 7: Reports Should Mirror People

Reports should *only* include information about those actions/functions for which identified individuals are personally accountable. Conversely, reports should include *all* of the information about those actions/functions for which identified individuals are personally accountable. There is no point, it seems to me, from an operating management reporting standpoint, to incur the expense and spend the time to gather and report data and information for which no one is personally, vitally interested!

But don't stop at the level of personal accountability. Management personnel are responsible and accountable not so much for personally generated results but, rather, for the performance results of the segments, departments, and functions of the firm which report to them. Therefore, there is an underlying principle to bear constantly in mind while designing the Reporting System. *Namely, costs/ expenses should be charged to and revenues (if applicable) should be credited to that segment of the business which is responsible for them.* What you should look for, to determine responsibility, is the power to accept or reject the invoice, pay for the labor, solicit the revenue, and so on.

RE 8: Incremental Management Applies to the Reporting System, Too!

Changes, developments, results in a business environment usually occur little by little, as we saw earlier. And recall, too, that we earlier agreed that it is always easier (and hence more likely to be successful) to complete small tasks rather than large ones.

Now consider a series of reports as a series of snapshots of the firm in motion. We all know that, just as in the case of the "real world," the shorter the time interval between the snapshots, the less difference can be noted in the subject from print to print. Similarly, the shorter the time interval between report issuances, the smaller the increment of performance change that will be captured. Just as in driving an auto or flying an airplane, correcting small deviations from the route or flight plan is always easier and more successful than trying to make large changes under crisis conditions.

The time period between issuances of reports is commonly called the "Control Cycle" (see Figure 8). So, to sum it up, this Reporting Element can be cogently put (and *not* unfamiliar by now I trust!):

> *The shorter the Control Cycle,*
> *the more likely it is that the*
> *generated management action will*
> *be successful—that is, effective.*

The Reporting Cycle emphasizes enhanced participation and communication. The form and degree of emphasis of

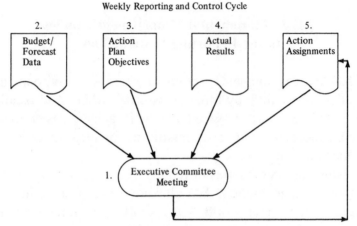

Figure 8.   Weekly Reporting and Control Cycle

each varies according to the control time cycle. The Weekly Cycle, for instance, centers on a meeting of the firm's Executive Committee—that is, the firm's president/general manager and those managerial personnel reporting directly to him. The basis of communication is the documentation showing the results of comparisons of Actual Results to Planned Results. *Communication* includes oral elaboration, face-to-face. Finally, communication of new tasks arising from developments are embodied in Action Assignments. *Participation* is also principally oral with across-the-table discussion. A surefire technique to eliminate all validity from an allegation that ''I wasn't given a chance to participate,'' is presented a little later as ''Two Questions.''

WEEKLY REPORTING

The major reporting and control role in the Monthly Control Cycle, however, is played by documentation. Usually, the only management meeting involved is the one in which the president/general manager reports to his Board, if we're dealing with an independent firm, or to his corporate superiors in the case where our organizational unit is a profit-center within a larger corporate enterprise. Please refer to Figure 8, which illustrates the principal ingredients in the Weekly Reporting and Control Cycle.

1. The Executive Committee Meeting

Too often it is the case that *a meeting is an event at which minutes are kept and hours are lost.* This weekly eyeball-to-eyeball session is the keystone upon which communication and participation rest. The Agenda is simple and always the same, as shown below. Each functional manager (head of marketing, of engineering, of operations, and so on) reports to the group, in turn. Interplay, questions, comments, etc., from all participants is encouraged, expected, and even demanded.

Executive Committee Meeting
Agenda

(For each attendee, in turn)
A. "Red Flag" items (any significant unplanned development, favorable or not)

B. Report on status/prognosis of progress re Action Plan
   Objectives
C. Report on status/prognosis of Action Assignments
D. Any new business the individual cares to bring up

Among the myriad benefits accruing from the Executive
Committee Meeting is the preclusion of buck-passing (or
back-stabbing) by the members of the Executive Committee. Pervasive publication of problems/plans/progress pro-
hibits politicians from practicing their ploys. This benefit
is particularly valuable to the new general manager. The
"new kid on the block" is usually susceptible to "snow
jobs." The heat of face-to-face reporting keeps the snow
from forming. It really *is* impossible to be devious in a
steam bath!

When the new or neophyte (there is a difference) general
manager practices bilateral communication excessively, the
subordinates are afforded the opportunity of playing Ping-
Pong using the gereral manager as the ball. You know
how it works:

MARKETING MANAGER: Honest, boss, sales would be higher if we could
   just ship our late order backlog. Is there anything you can do to
   break some of the production bottlenecks? [Ping!]
PRODUCTION MANAGER: Yeah, boss, I know the marketing guys are
   complaining. I could really crank up production if only the marketing/
   sales guys would give me a forecast so I have a reasonable time to
   get materials, etc. Why not talk to Marketing about giving me a
   forecast? [Pong!]
MARKETING MANAGER: I'd be happy to give production a forecast.
   But how can I forecast the planned new product? I can't get a release
   from engineering on the design. You know those guys, they're per-
   fectionists; they never want to let a product go. Better check with

them to see when I can expect it, okay? [Ping!] By the way, boss, our major customers won't give me a forecast until we ship what we already owe them.

ENGINEERING MANAGER: Sure thing, be happy to sign off on the release. All you have to do is get Marketing to stop changing the performance specifications. Oh, yes, remember the Quality Circles Program that you started in Production? That was a great idea, boss. You got everybody involved in quality and all that. Well, they have yet to publish the test spec's for the new product. Anything you can do to move them along will sure help—we can't release until after testing, you know. [Pong!]

And so on, and so on. . . .

Without a tool such as the Weekly Executive Committee Meeting, the general manager would be (and a surprisingly large number actually are!) worn to a frazzle just responding to the directives from, of all people, their own subordinates!

2. Budget/Forecast

This, of course, is the financial and operating data to which the operating organization is committed. They embody the sum of the Action Plan Objectives of the entire organization.

3. Action Plan Objectives

These are the specific, individual performance objective responsibilities which have been assumed by the management and other key personnel of the firm. These are the planned actions which bridge the difference between the demands of the owners/creditors and the run-rate forecast (see Figure 9).

4. Actual Results

These are the data gleaned from the accounting system and from the physical, real world of operations which measurably and quantifiably inform each relevant, cognizant individual as to how he did actually perform. The data can take the form of amounts, dates, and so on as appropriate to the planned action.

5. Action Assignments

If the fiscal year is a calendar year, the Budget and the Action Plan Objectives are usually finalized in October-November for the coming year. While extensive analysis and review accompany preparation of these documents, it is clearly impossible to envision all of the meaningful developments that will occur during the subsequent fourteen to fifteen months.

Action Assignments are used to control the management of these new developments. Typically, the characteristics of an Action Assignment include:

A. Name of the single individual to whom the assignment is made.
B. A brief statement of the task to be performed.
C. A date by which the task is to be completed.

No.	Objectives Description	Ref.	Responsibility		Fiscal Week								
					1	2	3	4	5	6	7	8	9
				Plan									
				Actual									
				Plan									
				Actual									
				Plan									
				Actual									
				Plan									
				Actual									
				Plan									
				Actual									
				Plan									
				Actual									
				Plan									
				Actual									

Figure 9. Management Action Plan Objectives

173

D. Any other quantitative measure which further defines the assignment.

All Action Assignments are touched upon each week even though the respective due date may not yet have been reached for one or another. It's possible that the assignment may have been completed earlier than scheduled, but usually that's extremely rare because the due dates tend to be set tighter rather than looser.

Minutes are taken and published to all attendees. Thus, the performance record builds, week by week. Each participant knows not only where he stands, but where all other management key personnel stand with regard to performance objectives.

Finally, end every meeting, *unfailingly,* with the "Two Question" communication insurance. The objective of management is to achieve predetermined performance goals/results. The objective of these meetings is to achieve economical, time-conserving, effective, and complete communication of (a) results actually achieved thus far, and (b) planned near-term action to either recoup a shortfall or exploit an unplanned opportunity.

So, even though the positive communication factors of Fixed Agenda and Fixed Format are utilized without exception, and leaving only the barest little to chance, every meeting should be ended by the chair asking each attendee, in turn:

1. Have you said everything that you *want* to say?
2. Have you said everything that you *should* say?

The chair, of course, does not allow the meeting to end until a "Yes, yes" response has been received from each attendee. Both questions are necessary. When the attendee answers "Yes" to the first question, he precludes the legitimacy of his saying, after the meeting, "I didn't get a chance to say so-and-so."

And when he answers "Yes" to the second question, he places himself in harm's way should it later be revealed that he possessed information useful to the management team but which he withheld nonetheless.

In short, all of the attendees have been rendered politically sterile. Moreover, the practice of politics will not only be fruitless, it will be fatal to the practitioner. Thus morale is improved, communication is enhanced, and management productivity reaches new heights so that return on shareholder equity can also reach new heights! After all, let's be careful to remember why we came to the dance!

THE MONTHLY CONTROL CYCLE

First, this cycle is centered on a report rather than on a meeting. Second, input from the Weekly Cycle is incorporated. Third, the managers/key personnel are required to not only recap results for the month, they must also look forward—*and* look forward quantitatively. In other words, each month, each manager/key person has the obligation and the opportunity to either confirm the quarterly, annual budget/forecast or change it. Fourth, each manager/key person synthesizes all of the new developments into a data sheet covered by a terse, concise, prose evaluation and outlook. This exercise in data analysis and reduction generates in-depth understanding and renewed commitment. Let's learn more about the Monthly Control Cycle.

1. President/General Manager's Monthly Report Input

There are four principal documents or sets of documents which provide the basic input for the monthly report. Each functional manager incorporates all four. For all participant/contributors below that organizational level, only the first two discussed are usually utilized.

A. *Actual Results:* These are the financial and operational data which reflect the actual results achieved during the month.

B. *Action Plan Objectives:* These are the same objectives referenced in the Weekly Control Cycle discussion. If the president/general manager is termed the first level, then all third-level and lower-level participant/contributors use only A above and B, as report input. Occasionally, they sometimes can profitably use budget/forecast data (D below) at least at the subaccount level consistent with the purview of their cognizance and/or control.

C. *Action Assignments:* These are generated at the Weekly Executive Committee Meeting and deal with unplanned significant developments which arose since the budget forecast was finalized.

D. *Budget/Forecast:* This is the third group of data against which the actual results are compared. The other two, of course, are the action plan objectives and the action assignments.

The forecast may change for the quarter or year depending upon the results of the data comparisons.

2. Manager/Key Person Report

The first part of the report discusses the results of the comparisons of actual data to objectives, forecasts, and/or action assignments. It is a prose presentation, concise, brief with incisive comment. Brevity has a premium. A restriction to one page can force mental discipline.

The data pertinent to the performance of the individual can generally also be captured and lucidly presented on one page. Shown generally are the bare data, actual and objective, and only enough prose to explain the objective.

Note that at each reporting level, the manager/key person can perform two tasks. If that individual receives reports from subordinates, he first reviews, writes comments upon, and then summarizes them. Then, in conjunction with his own management report input documents (as explained in the preceding section), he prepares his own two-page report. That report, with copies of the subordinates' reports attached, is then transmitted to his immediate superior. At each successively higher organizational level, then, all of the lower-level submittals are incorporated until, at last, the entire organization's reports are submitted to the president/general manager.

President's Forecast Summary: _____ ( ) Infavorable   President _____   Date _____

AMT △

	Prior Month				Year-To-Date				Current Month				Quarter				Year		
	Actual	FCST	Budget	Prior Year	Actual	Budget	Prior Year		FCST	Budget	Prior Year		FCST	Budget	Prior Year		FCST	Budget	Prior Year	
Orders Received																				
Net Sales																				
Commission																				
Net After Commis.																				
Product Cost																				
Total Variances																				
Operations Mgmt.																				
Engineering																				
Cost of Sales																				
Net Return																				
Administration																				
Marketing/Selling																				
Operating Pre-Tax																				
A/C Receivables																				
Inventory																				
Vendor Payables																				
Cash Flow																				
D/L Population																				
I/L Manufacturing																				
I/L All Others																				
Backlog																				

Figure 10. President's Forecast Summary

178

3. The President/General Manager's Report

A. After study and review of each and every submittal with written comment on them as he deems appropriate, the general manager prepares his report, his overview. It is his responsibility to distill the most important developments, findings, opportunities, and problems of the entire organization. It is his responsibility, further, to define the priority of action, to focus his organization's attention on those planned actions which are pivotal to total performance.

He must also explain and otherwise report on results as well as present his personal prognosis to the owners/creditors and/or higher level corporate management.

B. The data portion of the President/General Manager's Report is the Forecast Summary (ofttimes lovingly known as, "The Page of a 1,000 Numbers") which, for each key financial and operational topic, he either confirms the prior budget/forecast or presents a new forecast (see Figure 10). Clearly, changes to the budget/forecast require extensive explanation. Even more clearly, unfavorable changes require even more explanation.

4. Report Distribution

The Monthly Management Report, then, consists of the President/General Manager's Report *plus* each and every Management/Key Person's Report. The owners/creditors and/or higher level corporate management obtain copies of the Monthly Management Report as they may desire.

Equally important, a complete copy of the Monthly Management Report is distributed to each and every individual who submitted a report. *The communication loop is complete.* All excuses have been removed for lack of awareness, first, of each individual's progress and status, and, second, where the entire organization stands, which way it's headed, and what, precisely, are the shots that the top man is calling.

COMPENSATION

We come now, finally, to consideration of Financial Motivation: MONEY! Dessert is always served last, you know. There are only two types of compensation: ordinary compensation and incentive compensation. For our purposes, the incentive type of compensation is of prime importance. There are many very useful books available on how to structure, initiate, and implement Ordinary Compensation Programs. While incentive compensation is our prime focus, it is important to understand how the two types are interrelated and interdependent.

First of all, there is considerable truth and merit in the proposition that "If you do a really good job, your reward is that you get to keep it." And, up to a point, it does indeed generate some motivation. Usually, though, the motivation is based on fear rather than on pride. The difference is crucial. While fear motivation will result in some improvement of performance, the resulting action is always "to the letter" type. On the other hand, motivation which comes from pride is always of the "in the spirit of" type of action. We both know how painful it is to work with people who are interested only in performing "to the letter''—it's like trying to dance with a telephone pole! When people operate ''in the spirit of,'' however, their enthusiasm becomes contagious and winning becomes a habit.

Remember that my viewpoint is aimed at the vast majority, the more than 95 percent of management personnel (and those who so aspire) for whom money is a persuasive and compelling turn-on. What I will say about ordinary and incentive compensation is premised on the pervasive attitude that more money is always better than the same amount or less. I do not even try to talk to those readers in the less-than-5-percent group who rank the U.S. dollar low on their list of value priorities.

The focus of the balance of this chapter is placed on ''direct'' compensation. This type of compensation consists of money paid directly to the manager for services rendered. Usually, this compensation is paid from Payroll Accounts from which taxes, etc., are deducted or withheld. In this book I do *not* deal with ''indirect'' compensation, which consists, largely, of prerequisites such as insurance, pension plans, stock purchase plans, expense account allowances, and so on. Those sums are usually never paid from Payroll Accounts.

The basic purpose of compensation is to motivate the employee to perform assigned tasks more effectively than perhaps otherwise would be the case. The question inevitably arises, ''How much is the 'right' amount of compensation?'' The very best answer that I know of is that the ''right'' amount of a manager's compensation consists of a salary (ordinary compensation) that is (1) competitive in the relevant employment market, (2) equitable in relation to the job being performed, and (3) appropriately rewarding for the quality of the work performed. In addition, if the manager's achievements have a significant, direct, and measurable impact on the total results of the firm, he should receive additional (incentive) compensation commensurate with the scope, magnitude, and intensity of his personal favorable impact.

The Elements of Ordinary Compensation

The cornerstone of an effective Salary Administration Program is the Job Description. Without a well-thought-out, tailored, and complete Job Description, the manager has no reliable way of understanding what is expected of him. Job Descriptions cannot be too well prepared. Their importance cannot easily be overestimated. It is upon this basic, foundational document that the success of the entire Salary Administration Program is dependent. Let's see how the various elements relate.

The key provisions of the Job Description supply the data which are translated into a Point Rating. The Point Rating is important because it leads, in turn, to the definition of the Salary Range for the position under consideration. But more of that a little later. What are some examples of the provisions from which the Point Rating is derived? Some, only some, are:

A. *Knowledge/Training:* This includes years of education; years and types of experience.
B. *Contribution to Profit of the Firm:* Here we deal with and quantify aspects such as: Complexity of Duties;

Independence of Action; Nature of Supervision; Number Supervised; Accountability for Results; Impact of Errors on Profit; Opportunity for Disproportionate Contribution to Profit.

C. *Other Factors:* These include such elements as: requirement to work with confidential data; working conditions (extent of travel, etc.); and so on.

Usually, the higher the number of points, the higher the Point Rating, and, in turn, the higher the Salary Range. The Salary Range defines the limits of the amounts that the firm is willing to pay a manager for performing the job under consideration.

The Salary Range is not developed in a vacuum, of course. Systematic and periodic comparisons should be made between the firm's Salary Ranges and those of other firms in the same employment market for comparable jobs; this ensures that the firm's Ordinary Compensation Ranges are, indeed, competitive.

Salary Ranges are typically further divided into quartiles so that, for example, the salary for newcomers into the position is found in the fourth or lowest quartile and the salary for the most experienced (*not* merely longest tenured, mind you!) manager is usually found in the first or highest quartile. Those whose salary is below the amounts defined in the fourth quartile are traditionally called "green circles." The performance of these individuals is usually reviewed at very short time intervals—on the order of ninety days or so. The idea is to raise their salary into the fourth quartile as soon as they earn it.

At the other end of the spectrum are those whose salary

is higher than the defined upper limit of the first quartile; these are traditionally called "red circles." The performance review period for these individuals is usually longer than "normal." Often, the practice is for no performance review until the Salary Range itself has moved upward so as to include the individuals in the first quartile. The aim is to delay salary increases until the entire Salary Range increases so as to, in effect, erase the "red circle."

And on what basis does the entire Salary Range rise? At least once a year, as noted earlier, the firm's Salary Ranges are compared to those of other firms who compete with us for qualified personnel. As inflation takes its toll, the Salary Ranges of our competitors rise, and so, then, do ours. No surprise. The market sets the price. What's new?

And how does one progress from "green circle" through all four quartiles and into a "red circle?" By performing excellently, that's all.

How often should the manager's performance be reviewed? At a minimum, no less than every twelve months. REMEMBER: A performance review is just that; it is *not* an increase review! A "green circle" performance review period of, say, three months is not atypical.

What relationship does quartile position have with amount of percent of increase awarded? Usually, the lower the position in the Salary Range, the larger the permissible percent salary increase.

All in all, the design and administration of an Ordinary Compensation Program is pretty straightforward. It is, usually, more costly to initiate the program than it is to annually maintain it. Unless you're talking about the very smallest of firms, it *always* pays to install a complete Salary Administration Program. The more professional the basic Ordinary Compensation Program, the more likely it will be that the Incentive Compensation Program will be successful.

The Elements of Incentive Compensation

It is the professionalism with which the Incentive Compensation Program is implemented that will determine the ultimate extent of improvement in profitability which the firm will enjoy! After dealing with these Programs for more than twenty years, there are eleven purposes or objectives which, if met, will virtually ensure success. They are:

1. To significantly improve the enduring value of the shareholders' investment.
2. To significantly improve the flow of operating cash flow and pre-tax income.
3. To motivate management and other key personnel to achieve/exceed "stretch" performance objectives.
4. To reorganize and incrementally reward individual performance consistent with actual individual results achieved.
5. To commensurately reward exceptional individual actual performance results which meet/exceed quantified, measurable objectives.
6. To establish a "can do," winning attitude to consistently achieve new and higher levels of managerial performance.
7. To provide each participant with the ability to measure his own individual progress *and* be able to calculate his own personal reward as he earns it.

8. To enhance retention of qualified, high performance management personnel.

9. To establish a management communication system whereby a reporting Incentive Compensation Program participant receives a copy of all other Incentive Compensation Program participants' reports in the organizational unit.

10. To convince management and key personnel that (a) the firm does *indeed* recognize the worth, dignity, and professionalism of *each* individual, and (b) the top-level management of the firm is indeed interested in and aware of the capabilities and performance of each management and/or key individual.

11. To facilitate each individual's development of a practical, realistic, and achievable Career Plan.

As your Incentive Compensation Program is formulated and designed, incorporation of provisions specifically aimed at improving effectiveness will go a long way to achieve the levels of success that you seek. The thirteen Effectiveness Criteria that I have found most universally applicable are listed below. The effectiveness of *your* Incentive Compensation Program will increase in proportion and directly as:

1. Performance objectives are impersonal, not subjective, quantifiable, and measurable.

2. Quantification of individual performance objectives and corresponding actual results uses physical, real-world data rather than accounting-system data.

3. Each individual can accurately measure and assess his own performance, his own personal impact on results.

4. Each individual can accurately calculate his actual and prospective amount of incentive compensation.

5. Each individual exercises control over the determinants of his incentive compensation amount.

6. The measure of performance is as close as possible to the point of impact on the Incentive Compensation Program participants.

7. Goals and objectives are a matter personal and exclusive to each individual. Payment of incentive compensation should never be dependent upon "shared" responsibilities or goals with another so that payment of incentive compensation becomes more a reward for cooperation than for results.

8. Incentive Compensation Program amounts earned are dependent solely on an individual's performance and independent of corporate and/or business unit performance.

9. The provisions of the Incentive Compensation Program itself provide the elements of a relevant and supportive reporting and control system.

10. The number of performance objectives is in the six to twelve range; not so few that failure to meet one or two does not totally preclude incentive compensation payment, nor so many that measurement and reporting are excessively burdensome.

11. Potential incentive compensation earnings are unlimited. That is, there should be no "cap" on the amount of incentive compensation that can be earned by an individual as results exceed objectives.

12. The Incentive Compensation Program provides for both financial and nonfinancial rewards, is responsive to

the full array of an individual's motivational triggers or "hot buttons."

13. The cumulative and total effect of achievement at 100 percent Incentive Compensation Program levels results is, at a minimum, 115 percent of the results that would otherwise be acceptable budget levels of operational cash flow and pre-tax.

A very important point to remember about the objectives themselves is that they should always require higher levels of performance than those required by the Job Description used in the Salary Administration Program. The objectives should always contain performance "stretch." Objectives and the effort to reach them should always result in personal growth and development. After all, consider the turtle! He makes progress *only* when his neck is out.

Incentive compensation objectives, organizational tier by organizational tier, must be mutually supportive of and consistent with the total performance objectives of the entire firm. They should resemble a pyramid, culminating in enhancement of the enduring value of the shareholders' investment.

Finally, incentive compensation should *never* be viewed or used as a substitute for ordinary compensation and vice versa! It should be clear by now that the objectives, purposes, administration, and motivational aspects of each are separate, distinct, and mutually exclusive.

Administration

Figure 9, as we saw earlier, is the key document for Control and Reporting purposes. Let's make sure, however, that there is clear understanding of where the data that appear on that document come from.

There are only three principal sources. They are shown in Figure 3, Analysis of Change in Operating Pre-Tax; Figure 4, Analysis of Change in Operating Cash Flow; and Figure 5, Analysis of Change in Compensation Cost/ Expense. In other words, all financial objectives should be directly traceable and relatable to specific interstices in one or another of the analyses, Figures 3 through 6.

The proper administration of the Incentive Compensation Program needs, just as any worthwhile serious project, care, thought, preparation, and documentation. The basics are presented here and highlighted in the Control and Reporting section.

DISCRETIONARY COMPENSATION

Yes, discretionary! Even after all the talk about quantitative, impersonal, objective, and so on, yes! Sloma says there *is* a role for totally discretionary compensation! There will always be one, two, or a few individuals who, while not formally "managers," are key, nonetheless, to the achievement of the firm's objective performance results. It's been my experience that the array of "key" personnel ranges from the good, old "thirty-year" guy who knows all about all the key customers to the executive secretaries who usually serve too unheralded a role!

The point is that there is, indeed, a meaningful role for discretionary compensation. There are (and always will be) a number of truly "key" people whose contribution simply cannot be measured with objective precision. But just because an element of compensation *can* be discretionary does *not* mean that it is, or ought to be, arbitrary and capricious.

Even though arithmetic precision may be lacking, a letter of recommendation which formalizes an explicit description of performance in excess of Job Description requirements would certainly be enough to support a bonus payment. The reward is still based on performance, after all! It is not (merely) a Christmas bonus, for instance, where the recipients have no idea, control, input, or understanding of why and/or how much they might receive. Paranthetically, the Christmas bonus is probably the most prevalent example of owners' "psychic income."

In summary, a professionally designed Total Compensation Program (TCP)—usually THE most important management action to ensure financial performance success— incorporates and blends the three vital sets of ingredients discussed above. First, don't overlook or fail to address the Motivation Factors. Second, do ONLY those things which tend to achieve or accomplish the eleven Objectives. Third, rigorously test and retest your TCP against the thirteen Effectiveness Criteria.

It will not be easy—but it can be the most important Program you design and implement in your entire career. Please don't hesitate to drop me a line and let me know what you think and how it's going.

INDEX